W9-BJQ-880

Twayne's United States Authors Series

Sylvia E. Bowman, *Editor*

INDIANA UNIVERSITY

Allen Ginsberg

Twayne's United States Authors Series

Allen Ginsberg

ALLEN GINSBERG

By THOMAS F. MERRILL
University of Delaware

Twayne Publishers, Inc. :: New York

Library of Congress Catalog Card Number: 74-99535

MANUFACTURED IN THE UNITED STATES OF AMERICA

In Memoriam
Carl D. Michalson
1915–1965

Preface

FOR better or for worse the name Allen Ginsberg has come to stand for something in contemporary America. Twenty years ago, a few literary-minded people might have recognized him as a budding young protégé of William Carlos Williams; ten years ago, almost every literate person knew him as the Beatnik author of the notorious *Howl.* Today, we tend to think of him as the nucleus of a very nebulous attitude that has bloomed across the breadth of the land (and abroad) to which we have given the name Hip. The point is that Allen Ginsberg is now recognized more as a phenomenon than a poet. He makes news wherever he goes. He is the *Guru* for a whole generation of perplexing, disturbed, dissatisfied young Americans. Most of all, he is a gentle man—a point too often overlooked under the hoopla.

The task of this volume is to avoid the carnival aspects of Ginsberg's career as much as possible and to focus upon the question of his worth as a poet. This objective has required, on my part, a willful suspension of disbelief on some occasions, as well as a tenacious desire to try to see things as Ginsberg sees them. I cannot claim complete success on either count, but I can say that I have done my best to come to terms with the Beat attitude, which I believe to be essential for even the first step toward an understanding of Ginsberg's work.

As a result, the first chapter of this book concerns itself directly with the philosophical, psychological, and social facets of what in the 1950's was called the Beat Generation. The second chapter —which draws, as it were, an esthetic from the premises exhibited in the first—attempts to show that the literary theory of the Beat or Hip writers springs directly out of their special philosophical attitudes. From then on, in chapters three, four, five, and six, I deal successively with the major poetic works of Ginsberg with as much detail as space has permitted. The seventh and final chapter is a brief attempt to recapitulate and confirm some of the preliminary axioms established in the second chapter: how Ginsberg's work is a reflection of a continuing literary revolution. Finally, a tentative appraisal of Ginsberg's work as a whole is presented where, once again, this question appears: Is he a real poet, or is he a "personality" posing as the bard of the 1950's and 1960's?

Obviously, this study can hardly be considered anything more than a beginning. It is an attempt to compile sufficient information and critical guidelines so as to enable a reader of Ginsberg's poetry to have before him at least a perspective which may help him to understand the works as closely as possible on their own terms. Allen Ginsberg is still producing, and he has written me that he is in the process of working on a manuscript for City Lights Books which will "include poems 1960–67 & that shd be done soon; mss. of 200 pps. Indian Journals is with Auerhahn press at printer's now; & a collection of essays, manifestos, interviews etc is assembled for Random House next year [1968]."

Too many people have helped immeasurably with this project for me to give adequate or comprehensive appreciation. Specific thanks must go first to Allen Ginsberg himself for his helpful cooperation and for his permission to quote both from all his poetry and from our personal correspondence. I am also indebted to Professors Jean Loiseau and Jean Beranger, both of the *Faculté des Lettres de l'Université de Bordeaux*, for their humanity in affording me every possible consideration during my Fulbright Lecture year in France when the greater part of this book was written. Gratitude is also reserved for Miss Carole Frankel for acquiring special information and also for Monsieur Simon Copans, Director of the Institute of American Studies in Paris, who so kindly assisted me in acquiring necessary research materials. Furthermore, I would also like to express thanks to Professors Hugh G. Dick and Leon Howard, former colleagues at the University of California, Los Angeles; Mrs. Marcella Rightsell, who did such a superb job of typing the manuscript; and my wife, Mary Jane, who patiently proofread most of the chapters.

Greencastle, Indiana

Contents

Chronology

1926 Allen Ginsberg born June 3, Newark, New Jersey. His mother, Naomi, was a Russian émigré; and his father, Louis Ginsberg, a lyric poet and teacher in the school district of Paterson, New Jersey.

1943 Ginsberg left Paterson High School at the age of seventeen to attend Columbia University.

1945 Ginsberg was dismissed from Columbia for allegedly scrawling anti-Semitic slogans on a classroom window and for unbecoming remarks about the president of the University. He held several odd jobs including that of spot welder at the Brooklyn Navy Yard and dishwasher at Bickford's cafeteria.

1946 Ginsberg was a literary agent; a night porter for the May Company in Denver, Colorado; copy boy for the New York *World-Telegram;* and a reporter for a New Jersey daily.

1948 Readmitted to Columbia University and graduated with a bachelor of arts degree and an A – scholastic average; remained at Columbia for graduate study.

1948–1949 The beginning of a series of mystic visions of William Blake; first beginning in a sublet tenement apartment in Harlem.

1949 Four sessions of psychiatric counseling followed by an eight-month stay at Rockland (New York) State Hospital for psychoanalysis and therapy.

1950 Ginsberg was a book reviewer for *Newsweek* magazine.

1951–1953 Market research consultant in New York and San Francisco.

1954 Trip to Mexico and ultimate relocation in San Francisco.

1956 Publication of *Howl and Other Poems* by City Lights Books. Subsequent litigation over this volume led to an "obscenity trial."

1957 *Howl and Other Poems* ruled by the courts as not obscene.

1957– 1959 Ginsberg makes various trips to the Arctic, Tangier, Venice, Amsterdam, Paris, London, and Oxford. Returns to the United States and begins series of Poetry Readings at various universities including Harvard, Columbia, and Princeton. Eventually, he gives up these ventures and writes *Kaddish* in 1959. Records *Howl* for Fantasy.

1960 Experiments with Yage drug in Peruvian jungles and writes of his experiences to old friend William Burroughs. Has terrifying visions of a Death/God.

1961 Publishes *Empty Mirror* and begins trip to the Far East. Has meeting with Martin Buber and various Oriental holy men. Appears as actor in the motion picture, *Pull My Daisy.*

1962 Ginsberg appears in a second motion picture, *Guns of the Trees.*

1963 Undergoes change in his basic attitude toward existence as is recorded in the poem "The Change," written at this time. *Reality Sandwiches* published; also (with William Burroughs) *The Yage Letters.*

1965 European tour again. Crowned *Kral Majales* (King of May) by Czech students in Prague before being expelled from the country.

1965– 1966 Guggenheim Fellowship.

1966 Publication of *Wichita Vortex Sutra.* Interview with Thomas Clark for the *Paris Review* series: "The Art of Poetry."

1967 Appears in movie, *Chappaqua.*

1968 Publication of *Planet News* by City Lights Books and *T. V. Baby Poems* by the Orion Press.

Allen Ginsberg

CHAPTER 1

Ginsberg and the Beat Attitude

I *The Beat Mood*

ALLEN Ginsberg's collection of early poems *The Empty Mirror* begins with this poetic statement of the profoundest fatigue and hopelessness; but the mood is one that most of us can recognize as religious:

> I feel as if I am at a dead
> end and so I am finished.
> All spiritual facts I realize
> are true but I never escape
> the feeling of being closed in
> and the sordidness of self,
> the futility of all that I
> have seen and done and said.
> Maybe if I continued things
> would please me more but now
> I have no hope and I am tired.[1]

Not exultation, not the certitude of a life that has found comfort in the evidence of things unseen, the mood is that of a spirit that has long been besieged by doubts and has experienced a face-to-face encounter with the enervating specter of despair. "I am tired," the poet says, and in this weariness that the words so clearly realize for us we can hear the echo of the complaints so familiar to us in the twentieth century to which we have assigned the name "existential." Kierkegaard might have diagnosed the malady as the "sickness unto death"; Jack Kerouac gave it a hipster christening: "Beat."

"The word 'beat' originally meant poor, down and out, dead-beat, on the bum, sad, sleeping in subways," Kerouac has said. "Now that the word is belonging officially it is being made to stretch to include people who do not sleep in subways but have a certain new gesture, or attitude, which I can only describe as a new *more*." [2] People of all sorts ever since this description have been scrambling to define precisely what this "new *more*" is. A less than happy conclusion, for example, is that of John Ciardi, who asserts that "the Beat Generation is not only juvenile but certainly related to juvenile delinquency through a common ancestor whose beat name is disgust." [3] More hopeful is Dorothy Van Ghent's appraisal:

> The distinguishing characteristic of the Beat Generation is, it seems to me, the fact that they have a myth. The myth follows authentic archaic lines, and goes something like this. The hero is the "angelheaded hipster." He comes of anonymous parentage, parents whom he denies in the correct mythological fashion. He has received a mysterious call—to the road, the freights, the jazz dens, the "negro streets." This is the night journey or journey underground (Kerouac's title, *The Subterraneans,* is pertinent). Where he goes is hell, the realm of death, ruled by the H- or Hades-Bomb.[4]

One is reminded of the last line of William Carlos Williams' introduction to *Howl:* "Hold back the edges of your gowns, Ladies, we are going through hell." [5]

The non-rational approach to existence, which seems to be one of the most heavily imprinted hallmarks of the Beat Generation, receives its share of censure. "The hipster gives up society, gives up intelligence, and thinks he is doing this in favor of the emotions," says Herbert Gold; "but he has already, without making a decision about them, let his feeling seep away through a leaky personality." [6] Norman Podhoretz seems to echo this sentiment: "Being for or against what the Beat Generation stands for has to do with denying that incoherence is superior to precision; that ignorance is superior to knowledge; that the exercise of the mind and discrimination is a form of death." [7]

These unfriendly evaluations generally resent the threat that the Beat Generation poses to traditional notions of order and decency—indeed, to society itself. Gregory Corso's sympathetic parable of the hipster's mission does little to reduce the resentment: "The hipster dressed in ermine in the golden halls of the Beat Generation will be the slayer of society, it is told in his enthusiastic eye. He will sack society with his sword of old prunes, climb the fortress with armies of penguins and fly away with the daughter of society. He will wed the daughter of society, and throughout all the nights of their marriage, he will drive her mad with descriptions of her father." [8]

Perhaps Norman Mailer in his provocative essay "The White Negro" provides the most concise and the most fruitful description of the beat hipster. He calls him "the American existentialist," [9] which quickly comprehends the fact that the authentic Beatnik sees value in actions, in moods and in feelings, as opposed to things and logical causality. "Existentialism" is also an appropriate word because it alerts us to the inevitable truth that there is no *systematic* philosophy to be found in the Beat Generation. To be "beat" is not to be committed to a group of principles; it is to possess a certain undefined but, nevertheless, discernible attitude about things: it is to be hip.

As with "existentialism," the definitive boundaries of "beat" have been blurred both by the variety of attitudes that they have been called upon to enclose and by the notoriety that the popular press has brought to the term. The world is all too familiar with the "Beatnik," but it is less so with the philosophy lurking behind the beard and sandals. Basically, to be beat is to feel drained of the energy to compete. It is the bored fatigue of the soldier who has been required to perform endless, meaningless tasks—ones that have no point for him, no purpose. Like the bored soldier, the Beatnik feels that the demands of society are equally pointless and without purpose for him. Society represents an authority from without; the Beatnik seeks an authority from deep within his interior. As a result, from the social point of view, he is beat, tired, "fed up." He appears at first glance a grumbling malcontent or an irresponsible hedonist. But, from the personal point of view, the case is quite to the contrary. Personally, the Beatnik tends to regard himself as a pioneer, an explorer of inward reality; in this respect, he has much in common with religious mystics. The much-sensationalized use of drugs and hallucinagens only illustrates that the quest for inward reality has taken advantage of the resources of modern science. A sincere Beatnik might easily see himself as a jet-age St. John of the Cross.

Another reason the Beat Generation can best be understood in relation to "existentialism" is because both attitudes, Beat and Existentialist, seem to arise as reactions to the problem of maintaining the significance of the individual personality in a godless world. The spiritual vacuum in modern civilization created by Nietzsche's famous pronouncement that "God is dead" has been too easily filled by modern collectivist values that have threatened the quality of personal existence. The Beat Generation, sharing the view of Existentialism, sees the problem as a matter of defending human personality against the overwhelming pressures of conformity, competition, prestige, and respectability—all facets of modern civilization that measure worth by quantitative externals instead of by qualitative living.

The pejorative "square" appraisal of the Beat Generation—that it lacks values—really misses the point. For because the sincere Beatnik cares so intensely about values, he is what he is. The fact that the Beats often disregard conventional behavior by not dressing neatly, by loving promiscuously, by experimenting with drugs, by writing poetry and taking it seriously, by maintaining a studied disinterestedness in the face of society's demands—all this is their way of demonstrating—first, to themselves and, second, in an indirect fashion, to the squares—the hypocrisy and artificiality of accepted social values. It is their way of rehumanizing themselves through a total re-examination of what it means to live.

Many times "what it means to live" is rather graphically and shockingly demonstrated, as Paul O'Neil's account of a Ginsberg poetry reading attests. "At a recitation in Los Angeles," O'Neil reports, "a man stood up and demanded to know what Ginsberg was 'trying to prove.' 'Nakedness,' said Ginsberg. 'What d'ya mean, nakedness?' bawled the unwary customer. Ginsberg gracefully took off all his clothes." [10]

Certainly, we cannot deny that this and hundreds of other similar vignettes represent a strategy of extremes. Exhibitionism, we might say; but we would be only partly correct. Extremism can be justified by observing that there is no room for compromise in such a serious matter as the rehumanization of Homo sapiens. It becomes a question of the Kierkegaardian "either/or," and this decisive attitude of "you're-either-with-us-or-you're-not" permeates the whole spectrum of Beat activites. Even the Beat language bears this Manichean imprint; one is either "hip" or he is "square." There is no middle ground. The same holds true in epistemology: one either listens to the wisdom of his heart or else he is written off as a rationalist—rationalism being anathema in Beat circles. Even in literature the shibboleth is in force: spontaneous creation is supported against academic impersonalism; in fact, the Beats regard "the university" with such hostile suspicion that the situation reminds one of the familiar tensions between labor and management in the 1920's.

Extremism is a technique for foraging for what is real. Kierkegaard, for example, has described the Existential dilemma in terms of a man thrashing about above seventy thousand fathoms of water trying to stay afloat. The Beatnik thrashes also—with his language, with his clothes, with jazz, with poetry, with all his eccentricities; and he hopes that his wild gropings may fall upon something of substantial value that can sustain him. He thrashes about for an ethic, for a commitment, for a literary form; but he always recognizes that the thrashing takes place inside his being, in that area which Sidney Cohen has described in the title of his book: *The Beyond Within.*[11]

The incessant search for reality within is a quest for authentic existence. It calls for reconnaissance at the extremes of human experience more often than not far beyond rationalism. This concern for man's stake beyond the limits of the reason is the quality of the Beat attitude which makes it such a close cousin to Existentialism. Both are philosophies that begin with the individual personality and, therefore, place uncommon stress upon subjective moods. Again, Kierkegaard seems to define the situation best when he describes Existential truth as "an appropriation process of the most passionate inwardness"—precisely the view of truth that a serious Beatnik would insist upon. He would not, as the rationalist, attempt to *overcome* his fears, his guilt, his dread, his cares; rather, he would exploit these feelings in order to reach new levels of truth about himself. Moods are indices to his reality.

Obviously, a commitment to such a belief leads to the ofttimes embarrassing confessions that erupt in Beat literature. As a matter of fact, a glaring characteristic of most Beat writers, especially Ginsberg and Kerouac, is their celebration of intimate biographical detail which runs the gamut of autoeroticism, drug addiction, homosexuality, and the like. To the social conservative, theirs is shameless exhibitionism. To the authentic Beatnik, it is the denial of shame itself, a manifesto that nothing that is human or personal can be degrading. If this attitude seems uncivil, even childish, some consolation can be had from Blake's assurance that "the fool who persists in his folly will become wise."[12]

It must be quickly pointed out that the alleged foolishness of "hip" values often turns out to be sage criticism of the folly of accepted American practices. "At a time when sexual excitement by way of the media has reached laughable, if not obscene, proportions," writes June Bingham, "these boys and girls in identical tight pants and shoulderlength hair are signaling that the male and female secondary sexual characteristics are not that important; their form of address for one another is 'Man.'"[13] Other examples of Beat habits reveal similar protestant postures which too often and too quickly are dismissed as examples of mere bizarre faddishness.

The bizarre, however, it is just one more example of Beat extremism. It is a case of meeting the extreme impersonalism of conventional society with its polar opposite, and the obvious ethical fireworks that are ignited by the collision have been well covered by the press to the detriment of a clear appreciation of just what it is the Beats are about. As John P. Sisk has pointed out, the Beats have become "locked in a dialectic" with society;[14] that is, they have assumed the role of the non-belligerent opposition, meeting the rigid rationalism of society with deliberate irrationality. It is "non-belligerent" opposition because the Beat Generation has no interest in resistance, in crusades, in movements, or in any activity, for that matter, that remotely resembles fighting. The Beat is an indifferent enemy of society as it appears to him; he is "an enemy" because he is appalled by the ugliness of its materialism, the ugliness of its goals, and the emptiness of its values. He is "indifferent" because he has come to realize that he cannot change society—change can only come from within. And so, the Beatnik chooses not to fight. In the battle for social, spiritual, and esthetic progress, he is a conscientious objector. He plays it "cool"; he seeks to "make the scene" as best he can.

II *Disaffiliation and Death*

And yet, despite the recurring claim by the Beats that they are not out to change the world, that they merely disaffiliate from the "bad scene" of contemporary life, the inevitable ring of protest does echo throughout their work. Ginsberg's *Howl* is a good example with its outraged opening lines: "I saw the best minds of my generation destroyed by madness, starving hysterical naked, dragging themselves through the negro streets at dawn looking for an angry fix. . . ." The anger is there, the zealousness is there; but what makes it different from the protests of the past is that the Beat attitude is not interested in social reform—in making the world a better place to live in where all people can have decent houses and food on the table; the Beat protest is against the spiritual anemia that is a result, perhaps, of the successes of the truly *social* protests of the past. The Beatniks' is the only kind of protest possible, one begins to think, in a rich, affluent society. And their protest knocks against every smug layer of American convention with the full brunt of its antithesis. Where American culture preaches that cleanliness is next to, if not godliness, a high popularity rating, the Beatnik refuses to bathe; where convention insists that marriage and the home are the foundations of the great society, the Beatnik glories in casual sexual liaisons and flirts with homosexuality; where society places the bulk of its hope for the future in the hands of science, the Beatnik listens passionately to the sometimes confused murmurings of his heart. His protest is, in the last analysis, so radical and so complete that it almost ceases to become protest at all. The words that have been most often used to describe this posture are "disaffiliation" and "disengagement."

"Disaffiliation" and "disengagement" are uneasy words to a civilization of joiners where often the number of organizations one belongs to can determine success as much as intellectual or personal achievement. Britain's so-called angry young men are easier to understand than the American Beats because they protest directly against a social establishment that appears to exclude them from the privileges and opportunities of a society generally felt to be controlled by wearers of the "old school tie." The angry young men seek to change conditions; the Beats do not. They are not interested in social rights nor social opportunities simply because society, by definition, inevitably means concern for the many as opposed to concern for the one.

As Paul O'Neil rather bluntly puts it, the Beats feel that "the only way man can call his soul his own is by becoming an outcast." [15] They are not, therefore, reformers. Feeling the way he does, the problem for the Beatnik is not solved by institutional reform because, whatever the change, his dilemma remains the same. As a result, he chooses a third alternative which generally proves mystifying to social logicians: he disaffiliates, or "drops out" of the entire scheme of traditional civilization and asks only to be left alone. There is nothing remarkable about the fact that Henry David Thoreau is something of a Beat hero.

The question that this attitude poses is whether or not it is possible for Man—traditionally thought of as a social animal—to live an asocial life. The answer that a Beatnik or an Existentialist would give is no, for interpersonal relationships are in both cases too highly esteemed to allow a completely ascetic solution. These relationships are significant enough to formulate literary credos in a manner that Ginsberg suggests in his *Paris Review* interview. "I began finding," says Ginsberg, "in conversations with Burroughs and Kerouac and Gregory Corso, in conversations with people whom I knew well, whose souls I respected, that the things we were telling each other for real were totally different from what was already in literature. And that was Kerouac's great discovery in *On the Road*. The kinds of things that he and Neal Cassidy were talking about, he finally discovered were *the* subject matter for what he wanted to write down. That meant, at that minute, a complete revision of what literature was supposed to be, in *his* mind, and actually in the minds of the people that first read the book." [16]

The kind of interpersonal relationships that this statement reflects (which one can find throughout Beat writing) has nothing to do with the eighteenth-century conception of the herd. The "one" is not submerged *in* the "many"; much rather, it is released *by* the "many." The late Carl Michalson, although speaking specifically of Existentialists, described the phenomenon well when he said, "Social relations which are based upon existential individualism will be initiated in the creative force of personal volition. Which means when individuals come together, they will not lose their identity by social proximity. Their social resoluteness paradoxically intensifies their individuality. At the same time, their individuality will not jeopardize sociality; for their link with their fellow-man will not be based upon the tepid and irresolute assumption that birds of a feather flock together. It will be based upon the responsible resoluteness of an inter-personal fidelity." [17]

This view seems to be precisely the Beat one as well. "Disaffiliation" can be understood as disaffiliation from the herd for the purpose of making "interpersonal fidelity" possible. Modern society, the Beat writer would argue, by twisting interpersonal relationships into categories of competition, barter, argument, belligerence and violence—covering the savagery of it all with a glossy mantle of respectability—has virtually mangled the concepts of "self" and "neighbor" into grotesque hypocrisies which reduce "civilized" living to an immense lie. One of Allen Ginsberg's "visions," described by the poet himself, documents at least one man's awakening to this "lie"; and it is worth including at length because it probes so deeply into the rationale of "disengagement." "I was walking around Columbia, says Ginsberg,

> and I went in the Columbia bookstore and was reading Blake again, leafing over a book of Blake, I think it was *The Human Abstract:* "Pity would be no more . . ." And suddenly it came over me again, and I was in the eternal place *once more,* and I looked around at everybody's faces, and I saw all these wild animals! Because there was a bookstore clerk there who I hadn't paid much attention to, he was just a familiar fixture in the bookstore scene and everybody went into the bookstore every day like me, because downstairs there was a cafe and upstairs there were all these clerks that we were all familiar with—this guy had a very *long* face, you know some people look like giraffes. So he looked kind of giraffish. He had a kind of long face with a long nose. I don't know what kind of sex life he had, but he must have had something. But anyway I looked in his face and I suddenly saw like a great tormented soul—and he had just been somebody whom I'd regarded as perhaps a not particularly beautiful or sexy character, or lovely face, but you know someone familiar, and perhaps a pleading cousin in the universe. But all of a sudden I realized that *he* knew also, just like I knew. And that everybody in the bookstore knew, and that they were all hiding it! They all had the consciousness, it was like a great *un*conscious that was running between all of us that everybody *was* completely conscious, but that the fixed expressions that people have, the habitual expressions, the manners, the mode of talk, are all masks hiding this consciousness. Because almost at that moment it seemed that it would be too terrible if we communicated to each other on a level of total consciousness and awareness of each other—like it would be too terrible, it would be the end of the bookstore, it would be

> the end of civ . . . not civilization, but in other words the position that everybody was in was *ridiculous,* everybody running around peddling books to each other. Here in the universe! Passing money over the counter, wrapping books in bags and guarding the door, you know, stealing books, and the people sitting up making accountings on the upper floor there, and people worrying about their exams walking through the bookstore, and all the millions of thoughts the people had you know, that I'm worrying about . . . whether anybody loves them, about their mothers dying of cancer or you know the complete death awareness that everybody has continually with them all the time—all of a sudden revealed to me at once in the faces of the people, and they all looked like horrible grotesque masks, grotesque because *hiding* the knowledge from each other. Having a habitual conduct and forms to prescribe, forms to fulfill. Roles to play. But the main insight I had at the time was that everybody knew. Everybody knew completely everything in the terms which I was talking about.[18]

The vision of people "*hiding* the knowledge from one another" testifies to the Beat conviction that people are more real (and presumably better) than society allows them to be and also that collective society has an awesome control over people that transcends their individual wills. The truth about humanity—the truth that society obdurately censors—is shouted by Ginsberg in his "Footnote to *Howl*": "Everything is holy! everybody's holy! everywhere is holy! everyday is in eternity!" "Everyman's an angel!" (*Howl*, 21).

In these terms, it would seem, "disaffiliation" becomes a religious imperative. For the sake of authentic existence, one must retreat from the citadels of unreality to the catacombs of Bohemia where the angelic existence at least has a chance. This is the theory, at any rate. In practice, however, "disaffiliation" has often proven to be an insufficiently nourishing philosophy; at best, it could be considered a delaying tactic that has been inevitably interpreted by the enemy, society, as irresponsible immorality and rampant license. To a large extent, the interpretation has been correct, even according to the ambiguous standard of Beat ethics; for the sincere nucleus of disaffiliates of the original movement soon attracted a predictable following of dubious adherents—the flotsam and jetsam of society's fringes—who enjoyed nibbling at the periphery of the turbulence, feasting on the by-products of the turmoil. For these, the Beat Generation became a sanction for undisciplined behavior; and, armed with half-understood scraps of Zen and mangled slogans from Sartre, Berdyaev, and Celine, Beatniks fabricated a hedonistic lotus land that was every bit as bogus as the society they pretended to spurn.

The limited success of disaffiliation can be seen in the Beat literature itself where at least the gropings for "interpersonal fidelity" and the movements toward authentic existence can be seen. The alternatives to the ethics of the herd which evolved were, of course, predictable: the sanctity of personal freedom and the right to live one's own life without interference from custom or law. At the same time, it is interesting to see how quickly the ethics of Beat Bohemia fell into recognizable patterns. John Clellon Holmes, for example, has pointed out in Beat culture "a return to an older, more personal, but no less rigorous code of ethics, which included the inviolability of comradeship, the respect for confidences, and an almost mystical regard for courage—all of which are the ethics of the tribe, rather than the community; the code of a small compact group living in an indifferent or a hostile environment, which it seeks not to conquer or change, but only to elude." [19]

If Beat culture sounds reminiscent of the *comitatus* and the mead hall, so does the Beat attitude toward death. Beat writers reveal an enormous sensitivity to eschatological matters, but most forcefully in their insistence that some terms must be made with death. "If the fate of twentieth century man is to live with death from adolescence to premature senescence," says Norman Mailer, "why then the only life-giving answer is to accept the terms of death, to live with death as immediate danger, to divorce oneself from society, to exist without roots, to set out on that uncharted journey into the rebellious imperatives of the self." [20]

The power of death to authenticate life which Mailer implies is certainly another instance of Existentialism's impact upon the Beat Generation. The leering death's head makes it virtually impossible to take conformity seriously. To the contrary, it generates truth, as Ginsberg poetically testifies in the middle of an early poem "An Atypical Affair" in *Empty Mirror*. As the poet remembers a girl who had once proposed love to him and who died a few months later of a brain malignancy, he muses:

> By Hindsight,
> I should have known that only such
> a state of deathliness could bare
> in a local girl such a luminous
> candor. I wish I had been kinder.
> This hindsight is the opposite,
> after all, of believing that even
> in the face of death man can be
> no more than ordinary man. (36)

Living with death puts an individual on the farthest edge of existence where he becomes "more than ordinary man" if for no other reason than that the dialectic of life and death demands it. Against the stark antithesis of annihilation, made all too graphic by nuclear arsenals, the Beatnik must raise an equally formidable thesis of life; and this thesis of *life* must be a pure polar "being" stripped of all social slag and pure in its honesty. Such an obligation makes the ordinary problems of existence (subsistence, the rent, employment, marriage) prosaically inconsequential. Life, to the Beatnik, appears as a challenge to death; and it is no exaggeration when Norman Mailer makes the claim that the "unstated essence of Hip [is] its psychopathic brilliance." [21]

What Mailer means by "psychopathic" is essentially not much different from "existentialist." Both terms describe a man who is interested in "valuing personal authenticity more highly than scientific exactitude" [22] and a man who listens intently to "the messages from deep within himself." [23]

On one point the Beats and the Existentialists, at least the atheistic branches of existential thought, seem to part company: the issue of commitment. Despite the popularity of the words "disengagement" and "disaffiliation" to describe the Beat Generation, most of the serious members of the movement feel themselves to be intensely en route to a commitment of one sort or another. Ferlinghetti, for example, says:

> I am put down by Beat natives who say I cannot be beat and "committed" at the same time. . . . And this is where all the tall droopy corn about the Beat Generation and its being "existentialist" is as phoney as a four-dollar piece of lettuce. Because Jean-Paul Sartre cares and has always hollered that the writer espe-

cially should be committed. *Engagement* is one of his favorite dirty words. He would give the horse laugh to the idea of Disengagement and the Art of the Beat Generation. Me too. And that Abominable Snowman of modern poetry, Allen Ginsberg, would probably say the same. Only the dead are disengaged. And the wiggy nihilism of the Beat hipster, if carried to its natural conclusion, actually means the death of the creative artist himself. While the "non-commitment" of the artist is itself a suicidal and deluded variation of this same nihilism.[24]

III *Religion*

As Ferlinghetti points out, the Beat Generation writers do care. And the object and the character of their caring set them apart and imbue the whole Beat phenomenon with a kind of free-style religiosity. Jack Kerouac, for instance, goes to great pains to emphasize the religious calling that seems to be a concomitant of Beatness: "No, I want to speak *for* things, for the crucifix I speak out, for the Star of Israel I speak out, for the divinest man who ever lived who was a German (Bach) I speak out, for sweet Mohammed I speak out, for Buddha I speak out, for Lao-tse and Chuang-tse I speak out. . . ."[25]

If nothing else, the religious fervor of the Beat Generation is comprehensive; and perhaps Gary Snyder has been the only one daring enough to attempt even a brief analysis of Beat religious tendencies. He finds

> three things going on: 1. *Vision and illumination-seeking*. This is most easily done by systematic experimentation with narcotics. . . . 2. *Love, respect for life, abandon, Whitman, pacifism, anarchism, etc.* This comes out of various traditions including Quakers, Shinshu Buddhism, Sufism. And from a loving and open heart. . . . It is also partly responsible for the mystique of "angels," the glorification of skid-row and hitch-hiking, and a kind of mindless enthusiasm. If it respects life, it fails to respect heartless wisdom and death; and this is a shortcoming. 3. *Discipline, aesthetics, and tradition.* This was going on well before the beat generation got into print. It differs from the "All is one" stance in that its practitioners settle on one traditional religion, try to absorb the feel of its art and history, and carry out whatever ascesis is required.[26]

Snyder's categories are necessarily broad. They have to be, for the religious concern that is evident in the Beat Generation is highly ambivalent and encourages the suspicion that this movement, at bottom, is essentially a bizarre yet sincere effort to solve the problem of how one is to live in a world that admits the absence of God. Characteristically, the solutions tend to be extreme, anti-traditional, and intensely inward. The church, of course, is shunned not merely because it is irrelevant, but because it is an institution—a collective, authoritarian base that breeds the inevitable formal hypocrisies of all social organizations. To put it most simply, the church is "square"; religious sensitivity is "hip." On the occasions when the Beat writers do exploit Judaic-Christian concepts, they exploit them with a fanatical application that knows no compromise. "Everyman is Holy, Every day is in eternity! Everyman's an angel!"[27] bellows Ginsberg over the blare of a saxophone. The offense of all this to organized religion is basically its lack of discipline and its general disregard for traditional ethical teachings. Theologically, there is not so much disparity as one would expect.

The word *Beat,* according to its inventor, Jack Kerouac, means, among other things, *Beatitude.* It is characteristically Beat that the genesis of this insight, as he explains it, should come to him in an illumination:

> . . . it was as a Catholic . . . that I went one afternoon to the church of my childhood (one of them), Ste. Jeanne d'Arc in Lowell, Mass., and suddenly with tears in my eyes and had a vision of what I must have really meant with "Beat" anyhow when I heard the holy silence in the church (I was the only one in there, it was five P.M., dogs were barking outside, children yelling, the fall leaves, the candles were flickering alone just for me), the vision of the word Beat as being to mean beatific. . . . There's the priest preaching on Sunday morning, all of a sudden through a side door of the church comes a group of Beat Generation characters in strapped raincoats like the I.R.A. coming in silently to "dig" the religion . . . I knew it then.[28]

A more sensational religious illumination was experienced by Allen Ginsberg in a subleased apartment in New York's Spanish Harlem. So arresting was this vision for the poet that his spiritual-esthetic existence has orbited ever since around the experience. "I wasn't even reading, my eye was idling over the page of *The Sunflower,*" Ginsberg explains,

> and it suddenly appeared—the poem I'd read a lot of times before, overfamiliar to the point where it didn't make any particular meaning except some sweet thing about flowers—and suddenly I realized that the poem was talking about *me*. . . . Now, I began understanding it, the poem while looking at it, and suddenly, simultaneously with understanding it, heard a very deep earthen grave voice in the room, which I immediately assumed, I didn't think twice, was Blake's voice; it wasn't any voice that I knew, though I had previously had a conception of a voice of rock, in a poem, some image like that . . . simultaneously the auditory hallucination . . . the apparitional voice, in the room, woke me further deep in my understanding of the poem, because the voice was so completely tender and beautifully . . . ancient. Like the voice of the Ancient of Days. But the peculiar quality of the voice was something unforgettable because it was like God had a human voice, with all the infinite tenderness and anciency and mortal gravity of a living Creator speaking to his son.[29]

Assuming the genuineness of the experience and its attendant emotion in both instances, Kerouac's and Ginsberg's, one can perhaps see in these vignettes something quite close to the quality of experience that Schleiermacher describes as "a feeling of total dependence"[30] or what Rudolph Otto has called "*Mysterium Tremendum.*" Otto's explanation of the term is revealing:

> The feeling of it may at times come sweeping like a gentle tide, pervading the mind with a tranquil mood of deepest worship. It may pass over into a more set and lasting attitude of the soul, continuing, as it were, thrillingly vibrant and resonant, until at last it dies away and the soul resumes its "profane," non-religious mood of everyday experience. It may burst in sudden eruption up from the depths of the soul with spasms and convulsions, lead to the strangest excitements, to intoxicated frenzy, to transport, and to ecstasy. . . . It may become the hushed, trembling, and speechless humility of the creature in the presence of—whom or what? In the presence of that which is a *mystery* inexpressible and above all creatures.[31]

All of the symptoms of Otto's *Mysterium Tremendum* are present in Ginsberg's full account of his "Blake vision." The connection is emphasized in order to suggest a coincidence between at least one Beat religious experience, Ginsberg's, and the sort of religio-psychic experience that has increasingly become the matrix of much contemporary theological thought. Indeed, not a few of the theological positions implied by so-called Beatniks seem conservative when compared with recent thrusts made by professional theologians who have felt behooved to prepare a secular gospel for a world whose God is dead.[32] One poem by Ferlinghetti, for example, called "Sometime during Eternity" is rather tame fare after the "hip" language has been peeled off. It proves on close inspection to be rigidly orthodox—even bitterly so:

> Sometime during eternity
> some guys show up
> and one of them
> who shows up real late
> is a kind of carpenter
> from some square-type place
> like Galilee
>
> . . .
>
> You're hot
> they tell him
> And they cool him
> They stretch him on the Tree to cool
>
> . . .
>
> Him just hang there
> on His Tree
> looking real Petered out
> and real cool
> and also
> according to a roundup
> of late world news
> from the usual unreliable sources
> real dead [33]

"Real dead!" Society, it would seem from Ferlinghetti's account, has performed the post mortem on Christ, has signed his death certificate, and has duly buried him; and this act, say the Beats, is the sickness of the twentieth century—it has killed the spiritual possibilities of modern man.

One must be careful to avoid the impression that the Beat Generation is a Christian revival. It is hardly that, despite its flirtation with several enduring Christian concepts and its exploitation of Christian symbolism. The spiritual authority for the Beats comes less from Palestine or Rome than from the other side of the world: the Orient. The formal body of religious and philosophical thought that most appeals to them is Zen Buddhism because of its conception of the holiness of the personal impulse, which often is interpreted as sanction for doing whatever comes naturally. Every impulse of the soul, the psyche, and the heart is an impulse of holiness. Everything is holy if it is simply understood as such, a point which Allen Ginsberg hammers home through repetition in his "Footnote to *Howl*":

> Holy! Holy! Holy! Holy! Holy! Holy! Holy! Holy!
> Holy! Holy! Holy! Holy! Holy! Holy! Holy!
> The world is holy! The soul is holy! The skin
> is holy! The nose is holy! . . .
> Holy forgiveness! mercy! charity! faith! Holy!
> Ours! bodies! suffering! magnanimity!
> Holy the supernatural extra brilliant intelligent
> kindness of the soul! (*Howl*, 21)

This is a declaration of radical spiritual egalitarianism: a statement that nothing is profane and that therefore no human act is not of God. As blanket a denial of evil as is possible, it represents what might be considered a fusion of Western and Eastern theological attitudes. The Judaic-Christian dualism of Good versus Evil is obliterated by an Oriental relativism which neatly does away with the evil consequences of the spiritual pride which has bloodied the pages of Western ecclesiastical history. The contrast is illustrated by a poem that might be considered a companion piece to Ginsberg's; written by Ferlinghetti, it is called "Big Fat Hairy Vision of Evil":

> Evil, evil evil evil
> World is evil
> Life is evil
> All is evil
> if I ride the horse of hate.[34]

In this poem the consequences of a Manichean outlook are underscored by the conditional *if:* "if I ride the horse of hate." One might call this a Beat acknowledgment of the principle of *honi soit qui mal y pense*—the world is evil to those who think evil—to those who hate instead of love. The Western Church Institution, it is implied, can be indicted for promulgating the "Big Fat Hairy Vision of Evil."

The alternative to ethical dualism might be termed a sense of the natural balance of things: an appreciation not of good *versus* evil but of good and evil. In the *Hsin-hsin Ming* or "Treatise on Faith in the Mind," a poem attributed to Seng-ts'an, a sixth-century Zen Master, can be found the following words:

> If you want to get the plain truth
> Be not concerned with right and wrong.
> The conflict between right and wrong
> Is the sickness of the mind.[35]

The view represented by this fragment, that the conflict between right and wrong is an unnecessary and harmful concern, has enormous appeal for Beat writers. The basic corruption of the "square world," as they see it, is its compulsion to be right. This compulsion has done great harm in Western cultural history because it has insisted upon a perspective of ethical dualism in which Good has always been set in taut opposition to Bad with the result that men have suffered the burdens of shame and guilt that have been the most significant by-products of Christian psychology. Obviously, the shame and the guilt are almost overwhelming obstacles to any view of life that celebrates a totally positive acceptance of humanity. The doctrine of predestination, for example, is one extreme case where ethical dualism, coupled with the demands of logic, has produced a psychology that history itself has shown to be incompatible with the practical claims of human nature. Alan Watts goes one step further by supposing that "this metaphysical guilt is so insupportable that it must eventually issue in the rejection of God and his laws—which is just what has happened in the whole movement of modern secularism, materialism, and naturalism." [36]

IV *Zen Buddhism*

Clearly, the Western religious tradition is unacceptable by the Beat Generation because it presupposes an authority from outside the personality; because it imposes an arbitrary ethical system upon men which breeds competition, envy, greed, and war; and, finally, because the concept of guilt is inherently antagonistic to the extreme humanism which is at the heart of Beat thinking. The solution to the problem is simply to relieve the tension between Good and Evil. Zen Buddhism effectively does so, and in this quality is the secret of its appeal to troubled Westerners.

According to Zen, evil is not considered the natural enemy of good but its inevitable companion. They are sides of the same coin, and the proper stance of a reasonable man toward them is not one of pursuit of one and resistance to the other but a natural acceptance of the claims of both. A man consists of both good and bad things; to deny, therefore, part of himself through an arbitrary moral code would be to deny his claim to the name *human being.* The argument is really between what might be called a "natural humanity" and an "artificial ideal." The "artificial ideal," because it runs counter to natural inclination, produces a contradiction in the personality which usually reveals itself in guilt or psychoneurosis. Zen serves to eliminate artificiality and to sweep away the psycho-ethical tensions that have marked the courses of most Western philosophies. Life is restored to a natural harmony with the world; the staggering moral burdens of duty, honor, and "proper" conduct are seen as foreign accretions to the pure, effortless simplicity of human existence. "In Buddhism," says T'ang master Lin-chi, "there is no place for using effort. Just be ordinary and nothing special. Eat your food, move your bowels, pass water, and when you're tired go and lie down. The ignorant will laugh at me, but the wise will understand." [37]

For the Beatnik, whether he "is at the bottom of his personality looking up" [38] or is simply worn out by the moral, social, economic, and political competitiveness of modern civilization, Zen Buddhism promises a highly negotiable solution to his dilemma. It offers an almost irresistible satisfaction to his vague spiritual hungers in a number of obvious ways. Whereas so much of traditional philosophy and theology has stressed the disparateness of man in relation to the natural world—so much so that even the contemporary humanist Erich Fromm can speak of man as "a freak" of the universe[39]—Zen Buddhism offers the comfort of reintegration with nature. This attitude celebrates the "oneness" of everything: material and spiritual boundaries are permitted to overlap; the conscious and the unconscious blend; an armistice is declared between man and nature; and the *satori* experience—the awakening of man to a knowledge of his "inseparability" with the universe—is not a remote hope half-hidden in the shadows of eschatology but a very real, very immanent possibility.

Zen Buddhism also appeals to the Beat personality in two other practical ways. First, it avoids asceticism. The Zen holy man, on principle, is nothing out of the ordinary; and, as Alan Watts observes, "Here, for the first time, is a conception of the holy man and the sage who is not impossibly remote, not superhuman but fully human." [40] Sex, for example, is recognized as a healthy, natural human instinct and is treated with respect and understanding; Zen Buddhism does not repress sexual feelings or activities. Second, the "oneness" of the Zen attitude precludes the stringent moralizing that is all too evident in Western religious dogma. The question of morality in Zen is simplified to a fidelity to one's natural self, a position clearly above and beyond the usual categories of right and wrong. In other words, to be right is to follow one's natural bent, according to Zen; to be wrong, on the other hand, would be roughly equivalent to resisting instinct and to allowing an artificial standard from outside the personality to govern one's life.

The inherent danger in this Zen attitude is that it appears to encourage ego-centricity and ethical chaos. The only answer to such a charge would be the simple argument that in Zen the ego is submerged into the "oneness" of the universe which means that the Zen believer at no time considers himself as "something special." His ego is not self-asserting; and, to quote Alan Watts again, the Zen believer "sees that his ego is his *persona* or social role, a somewhat arbitrary selection of experience with which he has been taught to identify himself. (Why, for example, do we say 'I think' but not 'I am beating my heart'?) Having seen this, he continues to play his social role without being taken in by it. He does not precipitately adopt a new role or play the role of having no role at all. He plays it cool." [41]

Obviously, the philosophy of Zen can be easily exploited as a quasi-respectable justification for hedonism, bohemianism, antisocial behavior, or just plain doing whatever one pleases. To insist that the Beat Generation has not done one or the other would be ridiculous. At the same time, it is important to understand that, under the large umbrella of the term "Beatnik," there are many degrees of sincerity. For this reason, Alan Watts has written an article (subsequently published as a pamphlet) which serves as a kind of guidebook to help identify the various species of Zen enthusiasts as he sees them. The title of the pamphlet contains the categories: *Beat Zen, Square Zen* and *Zen.*[42] "Pure Zen," as Watts describes it, has no formal discipline because, as soon as its essence becomes codified into dogma, it becomes its very antithesis. "In "pure Zen," "nothing can be organized, taught, transmitted, certified, or wrapped up in any kind of system. It can't even be followed, for everyone has to find it for himself." [43] "Square Zen," on the other hand, designates "the traditional and official Zen schools of Japan, Rinzai and Soto, to which many Westerners do indeed belong." [44] "Square Zen" is "Pure Zen" systematized, and it has little to do with the derogatory connotation attached to the term "square" by the beats. "Beat Zen," finally, is the unique form of Zen Buddhism that has been embraced by the Beat Generation and which is of particular interest to the understanding of Allen Ginsberg.

The exaggeration of two aspects of Zen Buddhism seems to characterize the Beat version of the philosophy: the holiness of the personal impulse and the idea of the Zen-lunatic or holy madman. The sanctity of spontaneous impulse originates from the idea of the "oneness" of things; that is, the *acceptance of* rather than the *resistance to* the fact that the world is composed of both good and evil. To be natural rather than artificial is the supreme criterion; and the spontaneous impulse, unadulterated by reflection, becomes tantamount to a holy assertion. The literary consequences of this conviction are obvious but are discussed later.

The second aspect of Beat Zen, the idea of the holy madman, is closely allied with the holiness of personal impulse. The holy madman is revered because he deliberately confounds the rational —artificial—tendencies of his disposition and therefore comes closer to pure natural existence. In other words, lunacy is cultivated as a part of a long discipline of disaffiliating from the material appearances of reality and from rational, material thought patterns. One opens oneself up, as it were, to the larger interior reality by purposely deranging the senses which are, of course, the receptors of external "reality." Since LSD and narcotics are biochemical aids to this process of deliberate derangement, their popularity among the Beats is understandable.

The imprint of the Beat upon Zen is extremism. Whereas the traditional Zen Master is a supremely integrated individual, so much so that his quiet "oneness" with the world allows him truly to consider himself as nothing special, the adherent of Beat Zen all too often has a chip on his shoulder. If to Confucious it seemed much better to be "human-hearted than righteous," [45] the Beatnik tends to carry human-heartedness to a frenzy: love at times seems to carry the force of a military campaign. The recent phenomena of "Love-ins" in Los Angeles' Pershing Square and in New York's Greenwich Village suggests the contrast between the "nothing special" of the Zen Master and the hyper-organized hoopla of the Western Beat version. The Zen Master awaits his *satori* in quiet meditation, never pressing, knowing that to seek the epiphany deliberately is only to lose it; but the Beat pursues his *satori* with a torturous anxiety, often enlisting the aid of modern chemistry to bring it about.

What seems to give Beat Zen away is its very artificiality. Despite the insistent claims that it is *society* that is unnatural, it is often difficult to discern anything uniquely natural that the Beats have uncovered. They work too hard at justifying the superiority of their strident "I-don't-care" attitude. It soon becomes obvious that they care quite a lot. In short, one suspects in many cases that the Beat brand of Zen is phony—phony because it is treated as a means rather than an end. In Beat practice, the idea of Zen becomes obscured because it is exploited as a justification for some other way of life; and that "other way of life" is only, more often than not, a dimly perceived conviction that something is rotten in the soul of America.

V *Allen Ginsberg*

Allen Ginsberg, who springs almost bigger than life from the discontented matrix of the Beat Generation, is all that has been said of the Beats and more. His attitude reflects the same awareness of something wrong with America and with modern civilization itself. "When will we discover an America that will not deny its own God?" he asks. "Who takes up arms, money, police, and a million hands to murder the consciousness of God?" Beyond the localized disease of America he sees even more widespread cancer: "Recent history is the record of a vast conspiracy to impose one level of mechanical consciousness on mankind and exterminate all manifestations of that unique part of human sentience, identical in all men, which the individual shares with his Creator. The suppression of contemplative individuality is nearly complete." [46]

This attitude represents Ginsberg's general commitment to the broad lines of the Beat point of view, but there is more to Ginsberg, a dimension that has been measured best, perhaps, by his closest admirers and peers. "He is one of the prophets come back," says Ferlinghetti of him, "he is an old man perpetually writing a poem about an old man whose every third thought is Death. . . . He has buttonhooks in his eyes with which he fastens on to every foot of existence . . . he is gentle as the lamb of God made into mad cutlets . . . he is his own ecstatic illumination and he is his own hallucination . . . and he is the flippy flesh made word and he speaks the word he hears in his flesh and the word is Death." [47]

This description is of course a tongue-in-cheek one, but the biblical epithets with which it is larded point toward the distinctive quality in Ginsberg which gives him his peculiar flair, his individual style: the quality of the messianic deliverer. Ginsberg is the poet who understands his mission as a search far beyond esthetics into reality itself: "His eye fixes itself/on every stray person or thing/and waits for it to move/like a cat with a dead white mouse/suspecting it of hiding some small clew to existence." [48]

Some of the "dead white mice" that Ginsberg has played with have been of a predictable variety, and it is only necessary to quote a few of his public statements to suggest his general social concerns:

> Recent history is the record of a vast conspiracy to impose one level of mechanical consciousness on mankind and exterminate all manifestations of that unique part of human sentience, identical in all men, which the individual shares with his Creator.
>
> . . . . . .
>
> . . . there is a crack in the mass consciousness of America—sudden emergence of insight into a vast national subconscious netherworld filled with nerve gases, universal death bombs, malevolent bureaucracies, secret police systems, drugs that open the

door to God, ships leaving Earth, unknown chemical terrors, evil dreams at hand. . . .

. . . .

America is having a nervous breakdown. San Francisco is one of many places where a few individuals, poets, have had the luck and courage and fate to glimpse something new through the crack in mass consciousness; they have been exposed to some insight into their own nature, the nature of God. . . .

. . . .

The stakes are too great—an America gone mad with materialism, a police-state America, a sexless and soulless America prepared to battle the world in defense of a false image of its Authority. Not the wild and beautiful America of Whitman, not the historic America of Blake and Thoreau where the spiritual independence of each individual was an America, a universe, more huge and awesome than all the abstract bureaucracies and Authoritative Officialdoms of the World combined. . . .

. . . .

Only those who have entered the world of Spirit know what a vast laugh there is in the illusory appearance of worldly authority. And all men at one time or other enter that Spirit, whether in life or death.[49]

It may very well be, as James Dickey has said, that "Ginsberg's writings are of the familiar our-love-against-their-madness-and-money variety";[50] but the strenuousness of the social message when it comes, the passion of the prophecy, the terror of the "Flesh made sword," and finally (to borrow a phrase from James Scully) the "uncovering of a community" [51] often twist the stereotype protestant stance into something that merits the badge of good poetry. When this happens, when the religious visions and scatological affectations are swept aside by the power of the poet's basic humanity, then "the Allen emerges from behind the Ginsberg; the man breaks through the paper wall." [52]

Probably no one has been more aware than Allen Ginsberg himself of how tempting a morsel he has always been for the popular press. He is good copy; and, despite his understandable pique over the fact that the tabloid version of Ginsberg often distorts the real Ginsberg, he must realize that the exposure has not been all to the bad. For one thing, he has been read and listened to with an intensity that few American poets have enjoyed.

Of course, the inevitable distortion has been damaging to his poetic image. It will be a long time before "Ginsberg the poet" will be free from the popular image of "Ginsberg the Beatnik." After all, he *is* bizarre. He *does* attract attention wherever he goes. He also bears the responsibility for a gregarious honesty which compels him to speak naturally and without inhibitions of virtually every intimate personal detail of his life. This honesty, along with a remarkable talent for showmanship, inspires the suspicion that there is a good deal of hokum in the history of this man. The problem in arriving at a just appraisal of the man and his work is to make the proper separation—to find the pure "Allen" that does not always emerge "from behind the Ginsberg."

Biographical information available tends toward the hokum. Ginsberg himself usually supplies the barest sketches of his life such as the account included in the Donald Allen anthology:

> Born June 3, 1926, the son of Naomi Ginsberg, Russian emigre, and Louis Ginsberg, lyric poet and schoolteacher, in Paterson, New Jersey. High School in Paterson till 17, Columbia College, merchant marine, Texas and Denver, copyboy, Times Square, amigos in jail, dishwashing, book reviews, Mexico City, market research, Satori in Harlem, Yacatan & Chiapas 1954, West Coast Howl 1955, Arctic Sea Trip & then Tangier, Venice, Amsterdam, Paris, London, readings Oxford Harvard Columbia Chicago, New York Kaddish 1959, returned to SF & made record to leave behind and fade awhile in Orient.[53]

This almost haphazard catalogue of personal history could easily mislead us by its flippancy. If it is not altogether hokum, it at least shows us that the place to find the real Allen Ginsberg is in the poems: in the long autobiographical *Kaddish,* for example; but also in the short pieces which rarely evade the personal touch of their creator. William Carlos Williams saw the potency of Ginsberg's personal touch when he wrote in his introduction to *Howl:* "This poet sees through and all around the horrors he partakes of in the very intimate details of his poem. He avoids nothing but experiences it to the hilt. He contains it. Claims it as his own." [54]

To round out the stingy autobiographical data Ginsbert officially releases, one can rely on Richard Kostelanetz' description of the man as being five feet, eight inches tall, weighing about one hundred and fifty pounds, possessing a resonant bass voice, and looking younger than his age.[55] Of his high school years in Paterson, Ginsberg remembers thinking of himself "as a creep, a mystical creep. I had a good time, was lonesome; but I first read Whitman there." [56] He was seventeen years old when he entered Columbia University and was a member of the debating team, editor of the *Columbia Review*, president of the Philolexian Society, and an English major boasting an A– average. His professors included such notables as Meyer Schapiro, Mark Van Doren, and Lionel Trilling. During his time at Columbia he won several prizes for his poems; but, more importantly, at the university he met two people who were to influence his life and art perhaps more than any others: William Burroughs and Jack Kerouac. "Burroughs," Ginsberg claims, "educated me more than Columbia, really." [57]

In 1945, Ginsberg was dismissed from Columbia. The grounds for his expulsion were some unflattering references to the president of the university and also the more colorful incident where he etched in the dust of a dormitory window a skull and crossbones bearing an obscene, anti-Semitic legend. Later readmitted, he received a Bachelor of Arts degree in 1948, the same year he experienced the Blake vision. After graduation, he held a variety of jobs: dishwasher at Bickford's Cafeteria, book reviewer for *Newsweek* magazine, market research consultant, and reporter for a Labor newspaper in Newark.

Behind these facts, however, was a Ginsberg undergoing tremendous internal turmoil. Four periods of psycho-analysis and a stint as an in-patient at the New York State Psychiatric Institute only suggest the unrest that erupts in his poetry. "Everything I write is on one way or another autobiographical or present consciousness at the time of writing," Ginsberg has avowed. "Whatever travels or psychic progressions I've had are recorded there." [58] Unfortunately, although Ginsberg has never tried to hide even a shred of himself either in his poems or in his public appearances, he has been buried under an avalanche of sensationalism by the press. A suggestion of Ginsberg's despair over this circumstance can be appreciated in a letter to this author in which he writes: ". . . there is probably a lot that requires explanation or would be useful to younger teenieboppers who got the wrong ideas thru mass media." [59]

On April 30, 1965, Ginsberg was crowned *Kral Majales* (King of May) by the students of Prague, an event he has celebrated in poetry:

> And I am the King of May, which is the power of sexual youth,
> and I am the King of May, which is industry in eloquence
> and action in amour,
> and I am the King of May, which is long hair of Adam and the
> Bear of my own body . . .[60]

Happenings such as this invite the attention of the public, which is always hungry for novelty and caprice; but, underneath the press-agentry and the instant legend, the poet and the man are one, sincere and indivisible. A Princeton undergraduate, reporting a visit by Ginsberg to the campus in 1966, testifies to one quality of Allen Ginsberg which continually crops up in such accounts. "Students," he wrote, "who often sought him out to see if he was 'for real' . . . were charmed and converted by the obvious sincerity of the man." What follows in the student's account represents, perhaps, Ginsberg's finest triumph in his battle against legend: "At Princeton, Ginsberg has always represented everything pretentious and irresponsible in the arts, but after his visit many of his greatest detractors were left with shaken convictions and new questions." [61] The measure of this tribute can be appreciated when one compares it to Ginsberg's declaration of intent: "I have no formal ideology at all; these ideas I present to people to make them think about themselves." [62]

CHAPTER 2

The Beat Muse

I *Poetry, Philosophy, and Art*

THUMBING through a volume of Allen Ginsberg's poetry can be a bewildering experience for a reader accustomed to the order and tidiness of the usual anthologized verse. Even taking into account Thomas Parkinson's suggestion that "the primary problem of poetry is notation, through the appearance of poem on page to indicate the reality of articulation," [1] it is arresting to confront Ginsberg's unpredictable poetic line which sometimes squiggles in a quasi-emblematic pattern or spreads across the page in a kind of Swinburnian or Whitmanesque rush. Sometimes the lines form geometric figures such as squares; inverted "c"s; or even oversized, blocked-out words such as "Funny Death." Other times they conduct themselves with almost military precision. If it is appropriate at all to consider form as a structure imposed upon a poem from without, then one must concede that the only fruitful question to ask about Ginsberg's literary theory and that of his milieu is not what school or movement it belongs to but whether any established theory exists for either of them.

The traditional tools of literary criticism simply miss the mark so far as the products of either theory are concerned. It is not that these standards cannot be applied to the poetry, but that the application more often than not results in irrelevant conclusions which inevitably sweep aside the unique value that this literature presumes to possess. What one is left with, then, is the problem of finding an appropriate set of criteria for judging the poem—criteria which will allow us sympathetic flexibility with which to appreciate the poetry on its own terms. The easiest way to satisfy this need is to assume that the esthetic principle which governs the work is a generic outgrowth of the philosophic attitudes which underlie it. In short, one must acknowledge that meaning precedes and determines form.

Justification of this approach rests upon an understanding that the anesthetic pathos which has been dubbed "disengagement" requires a new, free-style mode of communication which, in many respects, is openly hostile to university-oriented formalism. It is hostile on one level for the rather mundane reason that traditional form suggests institutionalism which in itself is automatically repugnant to these modern poets. More profoundly, the hostility is a natural consequence of these writers' commitment to an absolute present which reveres spontaneity and abhors stasis. Traditions, institutions, and customs by definition represent checks on spontaneous impulses; hence, literary absolutes are anathema. The typical poet of the New American Renaissance feels that he owes allegiance to no authority other than the poem taking form on the paper before him. The poet must, to quote Ginsberg,

> live
> in the physical world
> moment to moment
> I must write down
> every recurring thought
> stop every beating second.[2]

From this description of the poetic process, one conjures up a picture of the poet as a kind of divine recorder. The "physical world" is his sounding board, and his heartbeat strikes against it so as to produce the "recurring thought." The Classical notion of the poet as maker seems quite beside the point here; what is suggested, rather, is the concept of the poet as diarist, an idea no doubt directly attributable to Walt Whitman. Just as predetermined form might impinge upon the authentic candor of a diary, so preconceived poetic form inhibits honesty and encourages affectation. One is reminded of Whitman's lines in "Song of Myself": "This hour I tell things in confidence,/I might not tell everybody, but I will tell you."[3] This is the technique of the confessional, and the confessor willingly gives priority to the catharsis of thought and feeling over the structure that the catharsis itself will hopefully discover for itself. As A. R. Ammons understands the process:

> The lines don't shape, predict, and limit whole-poem forms. . . . The reason is that external reality (time, place, event) dictates Ginsberg's means, so the means are outside the poem and, though unrecoverable, are more complete there. Certain things happened in a certain city at a certain time: a journal, or cata-travelog of accidentals. Opposite (for clarification) is the internal vision, selecting, transfiguring, making new and whole; the poet servant to the poem that exists apart in terms of its own reality. The unity in Ginsberg's work is Ginsberg in search of unity, so that the poems are fragments of the search.[4]

What Ammons describes is a poetic process which scarcely recognizes the existence of a conventional set of literary rules. No formal authority is imposed from outside the poem for the reason that such an imposition might constitute a distortion of reality. To put the matter bluntly, Ginsberg and those of his persuasion consider artificial formal structures as engines of hypocrisy. These devices too often hide mistakes, and they sometimes encourage poets to lie about the truth of things. Robert Duncan, for example, has ironically observed that "form, to the mind obsessed by convention, is significant insofar as it shows control. What has no rime or reason is a bogie that must be dismissed from the horizons of the mind. . . . Wherever the feeling of control is lost, the feeling of form is lost." [5]

Arbitrary attempts to intrude control upon the fluid spontaneity of feeling would appear to be the most serious threats to Ginsberg's idea of poetic creation, and the rationale behind this point of view appears to be more philosophical than esthetic. The philosophical concern with truth is understood as immiscible with the traditional conventions of poetry to the extent that such standbys as symbol and myth become dirty words in the lexicon of the New American Poets. It is precisely on this point of the validity of myth that Ginsberg's attitude can be seen as part of a much larger contemporary struggle to seek relevant truth, for his suspicion of myth is identical to the Bultmann-inspired program of demythologizing the Scriptures. The common cause of Ginsberg's poetics and Bultmann's hermeneutics is getting at Truth. Just as outdated biblical exegesis is in many circles seen as an obstacle to the relevance of Christianity in a secular world, so is outdated literary dogma understood by the Ginsberg milieu as a barrier to honesty. One might go so far as to say that the credo of Ginsberg stands in the same relationship with university formalism as the New Dispensation to the Mosaic Law. In both cases there has been a reduction of criteria to one simple query: Is it relevant and real?

Whatever connection is possible between philosophy and art in this situation can only be suggested by the final lines of Keats's "Ode on a Grecian Urn": " 'Beauty is truth, truth beauty,' that is all/Ye know on earth, and all ye need to know." Ginsberg brings the essence of this conviction up to date during the course of his 1966 *Paris Review* interview:

> . . . what happens if you make a distinction between what you tell your friends and what you tell your Muse? The problem is to break down that distinction: when you approach the Muse to talk as frankly as you would talk with yourself or with your friends. . . . In other words . . . there should be no distinction between what we write down, and what we really know, to begin with. As we know it every day, with each other. And the hypocrisy of literature has been—you know like there's supposed to be a formal literature, which is supposed to be different from . . . in subject, in diction and even in organization, from our quotidian inspired lives.[6]

The aggressiveness of Ginsberg's honesty is almost powerful enough to skim one over the rough terrain of the logic it presupposes—a continual problem when confronting Ginsberg. Stripped to its essentials, the statement seems to declare that, if a sensation, an idea, or a thing is true, *ipso facto,* it qualifies as literature. Observing this same tendency in other Beat writers, John Ciardi has dubbed the doctrine "the holiness of the impromptu."[7] Certainly, there is nothing new in this concept: Plato recognized the sanctity of inspiration even while turning poets out of his Republic, and everyone knows the zealousness with which the English Romantic poets guarded each inspired comma. The unusual feature of the emergence of this phenomenon in the new writers is the degree of faith they place in it as a method of composition. The assumption of the holiness of the impromptu as a literary device logically derives from a common point of reference shared by Christianity, Judaism, Zen Buddhism, and Existentialism: the Truth resides within, and reason can only corrupt the purity of Truth's first gush.

Alan Watts, generally a sympathetic reader of Ginsberg's work, raises what might be the most telling criticism of this most central principle in Beat art from a position that is philosophically internal to the movement—Zen. "There is, indeed, a considerable therapeutic value in allowing oneself to be deeply aware of any sight or sound that may arise," he says; "But this is therapy; it is not yet art." [8] This most vulnerable flank of the new American writing has proven to be open to sarcasm from the conservative front. For example, Ciardi—addressing himself to Kerouac's insistence that nothing should be deleted from a manuscript because "whatever you try to delete . . . that's what's most interesting to a doctor"—comments that this statement is "symptomatic of a narcissistic sickliness in all Beat writing. 'This is important,' it says, 'because it happened to sacred me.' The object seems to be to document one's own psyche on the assumption that every reader will find it as interesting as your psychiatrist does. Sorry, boys: I find it zany without illumination, precious rather than personal, and just plain dull." [9]

The type of rejoinder that a Ginsberg or a Kerouac would make to Ciardi's objection is predictable. A statement by that quasi-mythical figure of the Beat world, William Burroughs, can stand as a model: "There is only one thing a writer can write about: *what is in front of his senses at the moment of writing*. . . . I am a recording instrument. . . . I do not presume to impose 'story' 'plot' 'continuity' . . ." [10] But, to an academically disciplined mind, Burroughs' remark appears to be a deflection of the question rather than an answer. His reply bounces off the restraining wall of pure literary criticism and plummets to the bedrock of philosophy. Literature becomes communication, and what is communicated dictates form. The inextricable unity between method and meaning makes traditional literary criticism an irrelevant pastime.

In Ginsberg's work, for example, content and form are so mutually interdependent that it often seems folly to attempt a separation. Feeling, rhythm, religion, and many times drugs conspire in him to produce a vision which, by the brute force and honesty of its essence, bulldozes its way into poetic validity. The ingredients, moreover, often achieve a quality of wholeness that cannot be fully appreciated by technical analysis alone. In short, it is not merely a question of art *imitating* nature in Ginsberg's esthetic position but of art in fact *being* nature. The ultimate rationale for such a conviction inevitably leads to the ubiquitous assertion that everyone is an angel, and who would dare assert that the discourse of angels could be anything but poetry?

It is possible, of course, to place this new posture toward the relation of art and nature into historical perspective, thereby explaining the phenomenon in terms of cyclical reactions and counterreactions. Francis Golffing and Barbara Gibbs have attempted to do so with some quite plausible results. "Poets first *assumed* the virtue of their 'copies' of life," they reason,

> then *demonstrated* it by argument, then reversed the field (during the Romantic Period), placing a higher value upon the poem than on the experience, then gradually lost faith altogether, whereupon they took to making intellectual subtleties to shore up what seemed to them a crumbling position. And now . . . it seems that two things are happening . . . namely, that poets are seeking, in one gut-bursting effort, to finally break through that "fence" which has plagued them through the centuries and has become unbearable, and on the other hand they are, at the same time, finding courage to simply assert the value of poetry through the act of writing it.[11]

The "fence" referred to above is the dividing line between art and real life which Ginsberg prefers to define in moral categories as "the lie" or "hypocrisy."[12] It is manifest that his is no mere esthetic argument but one of the functions of literature as an instrument of moral protest. In the literary logic of these new writers whatever is, is not only right, but art—a viewpoint shared by the current proponents of "Pop Art."

In itself, this attitude catches the Existential mood of contemporary times, but it also raises a serious threat to the integrity of poetry as well as to a balanced appraisal of reality. If reality, for a poet such as Ginsberg, consists of passionately felt interests germinating in a loosely controlled subjectivity (the dependence upon hallucinagens and narcotic stimulants would seem to mark his rejection upon control), one cannot help muse a bit sadly on the priority that poetry has been assigned. One soon begins to suspect that poetry has been reduced to an avocation and that the real activity of the writer is a Faustian pursuit of larger and deeper truth which threatens to take him out of the voice range of his audience. Poetry of this sort which begins to take the form of garbled communiqués sent hastily back from the fringes of inward exploration, perhaps deserves the censure of Karl Shapiro's belief that "poetry that defends fragmentation borders on apocalyptic knowledge and insane knowledge. Poetry that defends the derangement of the senses, synesthesia, associationalism and the like, drifts rapidly towards a religious state of mind in which poetry itself becomes a religion and an art of prophecy." [13]

The truth of Shapiro's contention can be easily demonstrated by a few excerpts from Ginsberg's statements. First, on the issue of fragmentation, Ginsberg says that ". . . I had the idea . . . that by the unexplainable, unexplained non-perspective line, that is, juxtaposition of one *word* against another, a *gap* between the two words—like the space gap in the canvas—there'd be a gap between the two words which the mind would fill in with the sensation of existence. In other words when . . . Shakespeare says, 'In the dread vast and middle of the night,' something happens between 'dread vast' and 'middle.' " [14]

This defense of fragmentation through appeal to parataxis is not new; Erich Auerbach, who develops it at length in *Mimesis*, recognizes it as technique for discriminating between reality and myth.[15] Myth, Auerbach contends, contains no paratactic gaps; it is self-contained in its own artificially constructed universe. The artist's control has filled in the gaps so that there are no intrusions seeping in from the "real world." Biblical language, Auerbach further contends, continually exhibits gaps; and paratactic gaps are what lift the Scriptures from myth and demonstrate their historical reality.

These views seem to support Shapiro's point that "poetry that defends fragmentation borders on apocalyptic knowledge." The many critiques of Ginsberg's poetry that suggest his prophetic stance—not to mention Ginsberg's self-expressed debt to scriptural rhetoric—lead to the same conclusion. Certainly, the voice of the prophet can be heard in these lines from the end of part one of *Howl:* "the madman bum and angel beat in Time, unknown, yet putting down her what might be left to say in time come after death" (16).

Fragmentation, then, is exploited by Ginsberg for precisely the reasons Shapiro would condemn it; and this exploitation sustains one's suspicion that poetry for Ginsberg is a means to an end rather than the end in itself. Furthermore, the objective Ginsberg seeks through poetry appears more and more to be self-integration, a fact which leaves him open to Alan Watts's charge that much of Beat poetry appears to be therapy rather than art.

Is there a way, then, to satisfy the claims of both Art and Nature without violating the philosophical convictions which necessarily underlie one's conviction that they should either be held separate or be considered identical? One fruitful avenue of exploration seems open—one, in fact, which proves congenial to the three paramount attitudes that appear to inform the dogma of the New American Writers: Zen Buddhism, Judeo-Christian doctrine, and Existentialism. As the conflict now stands, the New Poets seemingly object to control on poetry because it inhibits spontaneity which they consider the proper medium for reality. The traditionalists insist upon control because they view art as a distillation or even an improvement upon raw nature which requires esthetic ordering.

Zen art provides a happy compromise with what it calls the "controlled accident."[16] In Oriental calligraphy, ceramics, and painting, the accidental running of the glaze or the random sweeps of the fine hairs on an ink brush often produce effects of incomparable beauty. They are not planned; they happen. But the situation in which they happen is planned with infinite care. The brush, for example, is made of soft hair in order that its fluid sweep on textured paper will calculatedly produce surprises. "In the Zen-inspired art of *Bonseki* or rock-gardening," Alan Watts tells us, "the stones are selected with infinite care, and though the hand of man may never have changed them it is far from true that any old stone will do."[17] In short, Zen art exercises control over nature through selection according to unsystematic judgment. There are no precise rules, and the artistic criterion is expressed in one word which translated becomes in English: "suchness."

Christianity also is interested in maintaining the naturalness of art, although perhaps this interest is not quite so evident as in Zen. The "suchness" of Christian art resides in its non-representational character; that is, like Zen art, it does not strive to represent some reality outside itself. Instead, in its best forms, it contains the reality it describes. "The most enduring form of medieval art, cathedral windows, even though depicting Biblical scenes," observes Carl Michalson, "are by intention non-representational, for they were not meant to be looked at, as tourists do with the aid of binoculars. They are flashes of light and color in the walls of the cathedral, resembling fireworks bursting in a night sky." [18] Likewise, Existentialism is artistically interested in the happy accidents of existence. Being unsystematic by definition, its concern lies with the oddities of life and nature which serve to illuminate human meaning.

The key words in this discussion, then, are "non-representational" and "meaning." Perhaps these words in tandem provide the best definition for "suchness." They are significant because they place the burden of control not upon abstract prior patterns, but on the presentiality of meaning for the observer or the reader. Meaning exists only in the spontaneous *now*—the moment of apprehension. Outside the immediate present—that is, in the past—meaning withers and dies. For this reason such dogmas at T. S. Eliot's "objective correlative," simply described as a mechanism for triggering a certain response, lie far outside the new literary esthetic.

The specific application of these generalities can best be seen in the curious "formalism" that our New American Poets employ. It consists not of symbols and myths but rather "frames" and breath patterns. The frames are simply arbitrary limits that are set about thoughts, emotions, or objects in order to draw attention to their meaning for human existence. Breath patterns serve to provide a physiological metric control upon experience as opposed, for example, to the impersonal rigidity of iambic pentameter. In Ginsberg's case, the most obvious illustration is the technique of the catalogue which he derived from Whitman. The strategy here is simple enumeration, for items are piled one on top of another until their accumulation gradually reveals a pattern that is often ironic. A good example is the Ginsberg poem, "In the Baggage Room of Greyhound" in which the catalogue of suitcases, trunks, and cartons stored on "the rickety structure of Time" (*Howl*, 37) charts the geography of human existence with all its uncertainty and tragedy. The same could be said of *Howl*, for John Ciardi has had difficulty in believing "that any man could put together [the first part] without revision as tight a catalogue as I find there." [19]

II *Recent Literary Influences*

Ginsberg himself professes an acute concern over the problem of form, for he was early influenced by the poet who can now perhaps be considered the chief architect of the modern American poetic idiom—William Carlos Williams. While Ginsberg's debt to Williams is most evident in the early poems, he shares with most of the New American Poets an admiration for the late doctor that borders on idolatry. That admiration stems from Williams' lonely struggle against the university formalists to create "with his bare hands" a new poetry in the American idiom that would be liberated at last from European influences. Williams was anti-mythical, anti-symbolic; and his method was once ungraciously described by Wallace Stevens as anti-poetic. If there is any meaning to the descriptive term "anti-poetic" in relation to Williams, one finds it in his total disregard for older traditions. He was interested in the pure and simple things about him. These were the proper subject matter for poetry, and his attractiveness to the San Francisco Renaissance poets can be seen in this statement from his introduction to *The Wedge:*

> Therefore each speech having its own character the poetry it engenders will be peculiar to that speech also in its own intrinsic form. . . . When a man makes a poem, makes it, mind you, he takes words as he finds them interrelated about him and composes them—without distortion which would mar their exact significances—into an intense expression of his perceptions and ardors that they may constitute a revelation in the speech that he uses . . .[20]

Freedom at last is what these words mean to the New American Poets of the 1950's. It meant, in the words of LeRoi Jones, a return of American poetry "to a great measure of emotional and intellectual hegemony among the world's poetries, after about thirty years of its representation as a patently unreadable graduate student verse. . . ."[21]

The enormous influence of Dr. Williams upon Allen Ginsberg and the poets of his group cannot be exaggerated. Consideration must be taken, of course, of the fact that Williams was of an earlier generation and that inevitable changes have occurred in the chronological transference of Williams' "poetics" to the 1950's and 1960's; but the substance appears to have endured. This influence can be seen by comparing a few of Williams' key pronouncements with those of Ginsberg and Charles Olson, perhaps the central articulator of theory among the New Writers. The essence of these poetic statements about prosody helps to demonstrate the direction that the new poetry attempts to pioneer: away from the stultifying paralysis of traditional academic poetry.

Of paramount importance was Williams' conviction that the poetic line was the basis of the poem. "The rhythmic unit decided the form of my poetry," he said. "When I came to the end of a rhythmic unit (not necessarily a sentence) I ended the line. The rhythmic unit was not measured by capitals at the beginning of a line or periods within the lines. . . . The rhythmic unit usually came to me in a lyric outburst." [22] One may compare this explanation of the rhythmic unit with Charles Olson's later statements on the same subject in his essay on "Projective Verse":

> . . . the syllable is only the first child of the incest of verse. . . . The other child is the LINE. And together, these two, the syllable *and* the line, they make a poem. . . . And the line comes (I swear it) from the breath, from the breathing of the man who writes, at the moment that he writes, and thus is, it is here that, the daily work, the WORK, gets in, for only he, the man who writes, can declare, at every moment, the line its metric and its ending—where its breathing, shall come to, termination.[23]

Where Williams speaks of "lyric outburst" as the determinator of the line, Olson settles on breath; but the distinction is purely semantic, for Williams elsewhere has written: "We are reminded that the origin of our verse was the dance—and even if it had not been the dance, the heart when it is stirred has multiple beats, and verse at its most impassioned sets the heart violently to beating. But as the heart picks up we also begin to count. Finally, the measure for each language and environment is accepted. In English it is predominantly the iambic pentameter, but whether that is so for the language Whitman spoke is something else again." [24]

Two things are evident from Olson and Williams: first, that the basic constituent of the poem, the line, is not a product of intellection but of the physiology of man—either the breath or the heart; second, that it can be seen that the form of language is not static but a function of place, time, and emotion. The conclusion of these two premises forms the basis for Olson's theory of "Composition by Field," which can be considered the credo of the modern poets being considered: "FORM IS NEVER MORE THAN AN EXTENSION OF CONTENT." [25]

Ginsberg's prosodic allegiance to these principles is manifest. Commenting on the genesis of *Howl,* he poses the question: "But how sustain a long line in poetry (lest it lapse into prosaic)?" He answers, "It's natural inspiration of the moment that keeps it moving. . . . Ideally each line of *Howl* is a single breath unit. . . . My breath is long—that's the Measure, one physical—mental inspiration of thought contained in the elastic of a breath." As an aside he adds, "It probably bugs Williams now, but it's a natural consequence, my own heightened conversation, not cooler average-daily talk short breath. I got to mouth more madly this way." [26]

There is a suggestion of apology in this last remark—the student justifying his unruliness to a disapproving master—which is an important clue to understanding Ginsberg's unique style, which tends to soar above the medial plane of a poetic theory which in principle he accepts. Ginsberg feels the need to "mouth more madly." He wishes to break through even the permissive, flexible control that Williams deems essential. But when it comes to *why* he must do so, Ginsberg's various replies seem spurious. "Well, I got a longer breath than Williams, or I'm Jewish, or I study yoga, or I sing long lines . . ." [27] he whimsically concedes. On a more serious occasion he provides a short history of his prosodic development: "By 1955 I wrote poetry adapted from prose seeds, journals, scratchings, arranged by phrasing or breath groups into little short-line patterns according to ideas of measure of American speech I'd picked up from W. C. Williams' imagist preoccupations. I suddenly turned aside in San Francisco, unemployment compensation leisure, to follow my romantic inspiration —Hebraic-Melvian bardic breath." [28]

The result was, of course, *Howl;* but it is possible to sense here a subtle shifting of poetic allegiance. A new literary credo has stolen into Ginsberg's convictions to rival that of Dr. Williams. The sources of this new credo would be impossible to catalogue comprehensively, but the principle influence would seem to be that of Jack Kerouac. Ginsberg's celebration of Kerouac can be found everywhere in the poetry and prose comments.[29]

Kerouac's "Essentials of Spontaneous Prose" has been printed in *Evergreen Review,* and a few excerpts may serve to demonstrate Kerouac's responsibility in drawing Ginsberg beyond the fringes of Williams' program. It might be noted in passing that Kerouac's theory of Spontaneous Prose itself draws heavily on Olson's principle that "ONE PERCEPTION MUST IMMEDIATELY AND DIRECTLY LEAD TO A FURTHER PERCEPTION." Kerouac, who deals with this subject under the heading "Lag in procedure," counsels: "No pause to think of proper word but the infantile pileup of scatalogical buildup of words till satisfaction is gained, which will turn out to be a great appending rhythm to a thought and be in accordance with Great Law of Timing." [30]

The relevance of this idea to Ginsberg is easily discernible in two closely connected areas. The first and most obvious one is Kerouac's sanctioning of scatology as a communicative strategy. Even sophisticated readers of Ginsberg's poetry are apt to be bemused by his seeming obsession with Anglo-Saxon vulgarity and to dismiss the four-letter words as an adolescent preoccupation posing under the dubious banner of reality. Kerouac's promotion of an "infantile pileup" of such words "till satisfaction is gained" suggests an artistic purpose, but the essence of that purpose is vague. One is left with the assumption that for Kerouac, at least, communication is easiest through scatology and, therefore, a use of such language speeds up the artistic process by not forcing the writer to think of a more appropriate term. This conclusion is not a flattering one to draw, but the obsessive language persists in Ginsberg's work, and the only non-psychiatric answer one has is Kerouac's justification of expediency.

The second area where Kerouac's statement is relevant to Ginsberg overlaps the first. "No pause to think of proper word" is a liberating phrase. It describes a technique for deliberately blocking off the discriminating intellect by sheer haste. This presumably leaves the field open for the heart and assures protection from the intellectual contagion wards of the universities. Ginsberg's first puff of this heady freedom was taken, so to speak, behind the literary barn. "I thought I wouldn't write a *poem,*" he said, "but just write what I wanted to without fear. . . ." [31] The full break had not yet come for him; a poem was still something separate from what he really felt and thought. He explains the phenomenon of *Howl* in his *Paris Review* interview with full scatological emancipation: "The beginning of the fear with me was, you know, what would my father say to something that I would write. At the time, writing *Howl*—for instance like I assumed when writing it that it was something that *could* not be published because I wouldn't want my daddy to see what was in there. . . . Though that disappeared as soon as the thing was real. . . ." [32]

The discussion seems to have almost the same structure as a session with a psychiatrist: identification of the trauma, confrontation with the fear, and the disappearance of the malady when the problem is recognized. Kerouac again seems to counsel this sort of deep exploration of the subconscious being under the topic "Scoping":

> Not "selectivity" of expression but following free deviation (association) of mind into limitless blow-on-subject seas of thought, swimming in sea of English with no discipline other than rhythms of rhetorical exhalation and expostulated statement. . . . Blow as deep as you want—write as deeply, fish as far down as you want, satisfy yourself first, then reader cannot fail to receive telepathic shock and meaning-excitement by same laws operating in his own human mind.[33]

Literature or therapy? Does Kerouac's conviction that the "reader cannot fail to receive telepathic shock and meaning excitement" hold up against fellow poet Ciardi's: "Sorry, boys: I find it . . . just plain dull"?

III. *Poetic Communication*

The criticisms that have been raised against Ginsberg's prosodic strategies have been largely drawn from a viewpoint that can be loosely called "traditionalist." In other words, one has constructed the outline of a debate which probably has no resolution since a common denominator is missing. Kenneth Rexroth, for example, has observed that "no avant garde American poet accepts the I. A. Richards-Valery thesis that a poem is an end in itself, an anonymous machine for providing aesthetic experiences. All believe in poetry as communication, statement from one person to another." [34] As soon as one assents to the function of poetry "as communication," many of the arguments against Ginsberg are vitiated.

When the primary function of poetry becomes understood as "communication," it is inevitable that a corresponding shift occurs in critical criteria. Authenticity tends to replace Art as the paramount value standard, and the critical tests one applies to poetry must accordingly be rephrased. For example, it is perfectly clear that scientific assertions are appropriately tested with the simple query: Are they true or false? By the same token, most practical issues are resolved by asking whether or not a proposal is suitable or unsuitable. The matter of the authenticity of a poem, however, is not so clearcut. Because poetry normally deals with the experience of human understanding, it necessarily must acknowledge scientific and practical tests of validity; but it must also meet tests of a subjective nature. Hence, poetic truth is not the same as factual truth; and the term "authenticity," when it is set up as a value criterion, poses highly complex problems.

No one can deny that it is possible to inquire if a poem is objectively true or false. Such questions as whether or not a King Arthur or a King Lear ever lived are obviously viable. It is also obvious that the answers to such questions have historical rather than literary relevance. Similarly, one can ask, as the courts of law have asked, if a poem such as *Howl* is suitable or unsuitable for the moral health or interests of the general populace; that is, if the poem has "the slightest redeeming social importance." Here again, literary relevance is of only a marginal concern. The suitability or unsuitability of a poem, however, can also be argued before a hypothetical court of esthetic standards, in which case the test might be: Does the alleged literature meet the requirements pre-established by the literary establishment? Here is where the New American Writers sense that the issue of authenticity is sidestepped once again. Their objection is that all of these tests overlook the heart of the poem—the truth it presumes to articulate about human experience. Thus, they insist upon a third category of critical inquiry, one which transcends factuality, propriety, and social suitability in order to ask the most significant question of all: Has a human experience been communicated in a meaningful and authentic form?

The phrase "meaningful and authentic form" is deliberately left imprecise because these poets insist upon their conviction that form itself must remain ambivalent. "FORM," to quote Charles Olson again, "IS NEVER MORE THAN AN EXTENSION OF CONTENT." [35] The authenticity or inauthenticity of a poem is tested against the poet's obedience to the poem itself and not against an alien literary decalogue artificially brought to bear as an absolute judgment for or against it.

Content, then, determines the form of a poem; and the authenticity of the articulation determines its worth. And precisely at this juncture one witnesses the interpenetration of the art and the philosophy of the Beat Generation. The New Poetry might be described as what John Macquarrie has called the "language of existence," which he defines as "a language that describes the structures of human existence, and the possible ways of being that belong to such an existence." [36] Since the organized structures of existence, as the Beat Generation views them, are chaotic, inhuman, brutal and, above all, meaningless, the poetry—which is an extension of this meaningless content—is forced to employ an authentic language appropriate to the raw materials of the existence with which it is concerned. These raw materials tend to sponsor what could be termed a "language of misology," which Carl Michalson, for one, contends "is a kind of mistrust or even hatred of language" [37] because it proves so impotent to fabricate meaning from meaninglessness.[38] Norman Podhoretz sarcastically makes the point when he infers that, for the Beatnik, "to be articulate is to admit that you have no feelings (for how can real feelings be expressed in syntactical language?), that you can't respond to anything (Kerouac responds to everything by saying 'Wow!'), and that you are probably impotent." [39]

Kerouac's alleged "Wow!" response to everything is significant because the language of misology, "like existential language in general, is emotive, composed of sounds of despair and disillusion." [40] Misology accounts for the ejaculatory scatology running throughout Ginsberg's poetry and confesses to an inherent skepticism toward language, an admission that language falls too far short of what it is asked to express.

Golffing and Gibbs have observed this same tendency in attempting to classify some of the strategies that the New Poets have employed for deliberately creating "breaks" in their poetic patterns so that reality can come in. True to the logic of misology, rational syntax or literary polish is at all points held suspect. One technique is to break down "the *logical* or *necessary* requirement of 'plot.'" Since plot is an artifice, it cannot be 'life.' A second technique listed by Golffing and Gibbs is to make "the poem 'occasional' in a new sense—a 'throw away' rough jotting." The roughness presumably equates with "the real." Ginsberg's comment that *Howl* was composed without thought to publication suggests his relation to this principle. A third technique—one perhaps most relevant to Allen Ginsberg—is "luxuriating in the private and sensational at the expense of 'plot.' The poem might be conceived as an orgasm, or a series of orgasms, expressed in words like 'Wow,' 'Bomb,' and nonsense-syllables, sputterings, pseudo puns (one where the second meaning has no relevance). The poet attempts to *do away* with the 'one remove,' the imitation. The poem becomes, or is meant to become, the experience itself." [41]

This language pattern is that of a society that has lost faith in language. Communication is attempted with words that "tend to be emotional explosions with no objective correlates." [42] On the positive side, one sees the emergence of apocalyptic poetry: not poetry *about* a thought or a feeling, but poetry as an event in itself. One does not wonder that the claim is so often made that Ginsberg's poetry is unreadable. Ginsberg would be the first to agree; his poetry is not made to be read but to be lived through.

IV *Prophecy*

One of William Carlos Williams' favorite maxims, "No ideas but in things," [43] was his way of expressing the conviction that a poet should *render* rather than *tell* the truth about things. Physical objects arranged properly in the machinery of poetic expression, he believed, released energy—evoked discernment. Charles Olson, following in the footsteps of the late doctor, expresses essentially the same thing in his theory of projective verse: ". . . the poem itself must, at all points, be a high energy-construct and, at all points, an energy-discharge." [44] In many of Ginsberg's best poems —particularly those in which he has exploited the technique of cataloguing objects for a dynamic cumulative effect—this principle has been followed with superb results. But there is a wilder side to Ginsberg that grows increasingly more apparent throughout his development: rendering gives way to rhetoric; and the rhetoric, in turn, yields unabashed prophetic verse. On this one-way street, there is no turning back; for, as C. E. Pulos reminds us, "The method of rendering instead of telling is inconsistent with the role of prophet that the poet has often assumed in the past." [45]

There are reasons, of course, for Ginsberg's movement in this direction. He has been strongly influenced by an assortment of Romantic mystics: Blake, Whitman, Christopher Smart. His own mystical experiences cannot be discounted either. A myriad of pressures both personal and derivative have nudged him from the position of the cool-headed and disciplined poem-maker, William Carlos Williams, toward a free-wheeling mysticism that celebrates deliberate derangement of the senses. More and more Ginsberg begins to fit Yvor Winters' description of the "pantheistic mystic" who is "more interested in the promptings of the 'subconscious' mind than of the conscious, in the half-grasped intention, in the fleeting relationship, than in that which is wholly understood. He is interested in getting just as far off in the direction of the uncontrolled, the meaningless, as he can possibly get and still have the pleasure of talking about it." [46]

There is, of course, Existential justification for this tactic. It can be argued that the only reality man has is "fleeting" and "half-grasped" and that the function of poetry is to communicate these inchoate evidences of humanity. Still, one feels on surer ground when he takes his prophecy from the Old Testament, and one wonders if meter (defined as rhythmic feeling) is sufficient by itself to hold poetry in trust. For a firsthand insight on this matter, one has Ginsberg's account of the process of writing a poem:

> Analytically, *ex post facto,* it all begins with f——— around and intuition and without any idea of *what* you're doing, I think. . . . But anyway, what it boils down to is this, it's my *movement,* my feeling is for a big long clanky statement. . . .

Question:

> So you're following that feeling and not a thought or visual image?

Ginsberg:

> It's simultaneous. The poetry generally is like a rhythmic articulation of feeling. The feeling is like an impulse that rises within—just like sexual impulses, say. . . . It's a feeling that begins somewhere in the pit of the stomach and rises up forward in the breast and then comes out through the mouth and ears, and comes forth a croon or a groan or a sigh. . . . Or actually what happens is . . . there's a definite body rhythm that has no definite words, or may

> have one or two words attached to it, one or two key words attached to it. And then, in writing it down, it's simply by a process of association that I find what the rest of the statement is—what can be collected around that word. . . .
>
> Usually during the composition, step by step, word by word and adjective by adjective, if it's at all spontaneous, I don't know whether it even makes sense sometimes. Sometimes I do know it makes complete sense, and I start crying. Because I'm hitting some area which is absolutely true. And in that sense . . . understandable universally. In that sense able to survive through time—in that sense to be read by somebody and wept to, maybe, centuries later. In that sense prophecy, because it touches a common key . . .[47]

Ginsberg is not a maker of poems, if this account is accurate, but an instrument of spiritual communication. His is more than the case of a man indulging in "a poetry of confession in the absence of what used to be called discipline";[48] for the term "confession" cannot be strained to include elements in this account that properly adhere to the exegetical terms: "kerygma," "hermeneutics," and even "speaking in tongue." Even the word "mysticism," in its formal definition, fails to do justice to the phenomenon that Ginsberg describes simply because one is almost overwhelmed by the enormity of the ego lurking behind his words. Mysticism involves the annihilation of ego in communion with the Holy. As deliverer of the kerygma to men centuries in the future, Ginsberg tends to accept his self-assigned role of prophet far too seriously, and he thereby makes himself vulnerable to the observation of Karl Shapiro that, "when the poet feels that he is experiencing history or the universe, you may be sure he is about to make a fool of himself. The good poet sticks to his real loves, those within the realm of probability. He never tries to hold hands with God or the human race." [49]

One feels hesitant, even a bit guilty, in presuming to criticize the mode of another's quest for authenticity—even when the quest becomes chronicled in a form that literary tradition has declared "fair game." The unique problem with Ginsberg's work is that the quest and the poetry are married in subjectivity. To apply objective standards, to expose his poetry to the traditional yardsticks of "criticism," is, one feels, to smother whatever worth this material may have under a blanket of irrelevancy. There will be those, of course, who because of conviction will be unwilling to accept what amounts to an Existential premise in reading Ginsberg. To these, Ginsberg will forever remain, at best, irrelevant and, at worse, a literary *poseur*. For some, however, it may be the case that—if to understand is not altogether to forgive—it is at least to appreciate that, along with William Carlos Williams, Ginsberg "proves to us, in spite of the most debasing experiences that life can offer a man, the spirit of love survives to ennoble our lives if we have the wit and the courage and the faith—and the art! to persist." [50]

CHAPTER 3

Empty Mirror

I *Art and Honesty*

LOUIS Untermeyer was once quoted as saying, "The test, of course, of a great painting is do you want to look at it again? Or a great piece of music, do you want to hear it again? I have not read a piece of beatnik poetry that I have wanted to . . . re-read." [1] Mr. Untermeyer was not being perverse nor even unsympathetic in this statement; he was simply recording a natural response to an inherent quality of Beat literature which is its professed métier. For, as Untermeyer himself adds, the poetry is "tremendously exciting, tremendously reflecting the discomfort and the tension and the terror of our time." But can poetry be "tremendously exciting" and, at the same time, not worth a second reading?

The answer to this question can be sought by means of two approaches. First, the avowed principle of much Beat poetry is spontaneity; it attempts to capture the immediacy of the felt moment. Surely, one may question whether or not such a fragile thing as a naked, felt moment can support secondary or tertiary scrutiny unless it depends upon formal, esthetic support. Certainly it is true, as Rossetti has declared, that a sonnet is a "moment's monument";[2] but it is also true that some moments, even though they evoke significant reality, are decidedly unpleasant, and their value resides more in the truth they discover than in the beauty they excite. The equation that Beatnik poets tend to see between truth and beauty complicates the problem unless we are willing to accept their poetry on its own terms. Their terms lead us to the second approach to the paradox, which acknowledges that art need not be restricted to the traditional boundary lines of beauty but can be defended in terms of revelation.

No one would quarrel with the assertion that human nature

does not enjoy sustained immersion in ugly truth. While man may find it "tremendously exciting" to experience ugly truth momentarily, he also finds that a steady diet of life without illusion ceases to be exhilarating. Beat poetry makes many people uncomfortable because it exposes a side of themselves that they prefer to ignore. This poetry is akin to what Paul Tillich speaks of when he contends that "modern art is not propaganda but revelation. It shows that the reality of our existence is as it is. It does not cover up the reality in which we are living. The question therefore is this: Is the revelation of a situation propaganda for it? If this were the case all art would have to become dishonest beautification." [3]

There is no propaganda in Ginsberg's poetic revelations nor is there beautification. In this volume of early poems, *Empty Mirror*, one finds, as William Carlos Williams points out in the introduction,

> a new sort of line, omitting memories of trees and watercourses and clouds and pleasant glades. . . . It is measured by the passage of time without accent, monotonous, useless—unless you are drawn as Dante to see the truth, undressed, and to sway to a beat that is far removed from the beat of dancing feet but rather finds in the shuffling of human beings in all the stages of their day, the trip to the bathroom, to the stairs of the subway, the steps of the office or factory routine the mystical measure of the passions. (5)

The moments that Williams lists are not the sort that one usually immortalizes with a monument, but they are very much a part of the poetry of human existence. Ginsberg's poems are not *objets d'art;* they are eruptions of anguish.

The word "anguish" itself, perhaps better than any other single term, describes the basic concerns of Ginsberg's poetry; for, if one heeds the words of Nikolai Berdyaev, anguish "is always evidence of longing for eternity, of inability to come to terms with time." Berdyaev also says that "When we face the future we are moved not only by hope but also by anguish; for, in the end, the future carries death within itself and thus gives rise to anguish." [4] Inevitably, anguish also reflects an inability to answer the question: Who am I? The experience of looking into a mirror and seeing no reflection inspires the title of this volume of poetry: *Empty Mirror.*

II *Mind and Body*

Most of the poems in this collection were written between 1947 and 1952 when Ginsberg was in his early twenties, but they already represent a serious crisis that most men never encounter in a lifetime. The first poetic rendering of this crisis has already been examined in Chapter 1. The lethargic mood of despair of "I have no hope and I am tired," continued on the next page of *Empty Mirror* (8), makes one feel that one is led down a dark cul-de-sac of forlorn existence. "Tonite all is well," one reads; but this assurance is immediately vitiated by the poet's resignation to a hopeless road ahead; "What a terrible future," he sadly predicts. Ginsberg, twenty-three (the "year of the iron birthday"), regards the anniversary as a "gate of darkness."

Chronology is merely a metaphor in the context of this poem. The birthday is, of course, a convenient occasion for personal assessment; but the real subject is illness. The poet, "spiritually and physically impotent" in the midst of a month of "madness," makes it quite clear that things cannot continue as they have. The scene is set for some necessary event, for some "cue for passion" to occur to break the mood; for no one can continue in anguish without some resolve, some salutary change, or some event which will produce an image in the mirror.

What are the options open to such a distressed soul? Because Ginsberg outlines in his poem an almost classic Existential predicament, they are not difficult to list. Hamlet has been over this road before Ginsberg, and the path is well-worn. There is always suicide ("To be or not to be . . ."), but even Hamlet dismisses this option before he seriously considers it. For Ginsberg, the objection to suicide is not the fear of some "undiscovered country" [5] but the ignominy of capitulation. Suicide would represent a cowardly rejection of what Paul Tillich has called the "courage to be." [6]

Another option is Albert Camus's proposal of an irrational affirmation of life in the face of death. This strategy is illustrated in the myth of Sisyphus where "Sisyphus, who despite being condemned to ceaselessly roll a rock to the top of a mountain only to have it fall back of its own weight, nevertheless not only endures but also finds joy in this task." [7] A third alternative would be a spiritual withdrawal from worldly activity which, according to Berdyaev, is decisively encouraged by anguish. "Anguish," he has confessed, "has persistently weakened my activity in the world: I thought to withdraw." [8]

This third option, seemingly the one Ginsberg elects in his poem, is expressed in an extreme commitment to platonic dualism:

> I suddenly realized that my head
> is severed from my body;
> I realized it a few nights ago
> by myself
> lying sleepless on the couch. (8)

The withdrawal implicit in these lines suggests an inchoate mysticism. Ginsberg seems to be documenting his resolution to pursue his "real" existence in the mind—to bifurcate living; that is, to ignore the body, as far as authentic existence is concerned, and to realize his destiny solely in the mind and in the spirit. In these terms, his is a crude first step along the mystic way, a conclusion which gains support from the fact that the experience documented in this poem occurred after Ginsberg had had his Blake vision at which time he had vowed: ". . . this was what I was born for . . . never forget, never renig [*sic.*], never deny. Never deny the voice—no, never *forget* it, don't get lost mentally wandering in other spirit worlds or American job worlds or advertising worlds or war worlds or earth worlds." [9] In short, the resolution described in this poem was a *fait accompli* at the time he wrote it.

The significance of this poem in terms of Ginsberg's literary development transcends by far its merit as poetry because it marks the beginning of a cycle starting with the Blake vision and ending on a Japanese train in 1963 when he wrote "The Change." What transpired in the interim was a metaphysical journey in search of reality through various levels of consciousness outside the body. The direction of this search finally took a dramatic turn after a series of conversations with holy men in India and with contemporary theologians such as Martin Buber. What Ginsberg learned from these conversations was that the vital area for seeking reality was within the self. As Ginsberg himself explains, the problem was "getting *in* the body rather than getting out of the human form."[10] Speaking of his talks with Buber, Ginsberg says: "I was thinking like loss of identity and confrontation with non-human universe as the main problem, and in a sense whether or not man had to evolve and change, and perhaps become non-human too. Melt into the universe, let us say. . . . Buber said that he was interested in man-to-man relationships, human-to-human."[11]

The severance of head from body in this very early poem is, therefore, a definite departure point that helps one navigate the tortuous course of Ginsberg's philosophical progress with a bit more clarity. For example, the consequence of a man's mind being led by anguish from the human world into the supermundane is documented in another early poem contained in *Empty Mirror:* "I have Increased Power." In this poem Ginsberg diagnoses his own symptoms after having followed his "mystic way" for some time.

> Trouble with
> me now, no active life
> in realworld. And Time,
> as realworld, appearing vile,
> as Shakespeare says:
> ruinous, vile, dirty Time. (23)

This realization, which seems to be almost identical to that of Berdyaev, is not only similar to his confession that "anguish has persistently weakened my activity in the world," but also very close to his conviction that anguish "drives man toward the transcendent; while creativity is that very movement towards transcendence and the evocation of the image of the wholly other in relation to this life."[12] Ginsberg's "Psalm I" (9)—with its rather exotic references to "the vision haunted mind," "the majestic flaws of mind," and the anticipated descent of the Dove—only suggests the close correspondence his experience has to that of Berdyaev.

Ginsberg, in fact, has written a series of psalms; there are three in all: the second was published in fragmentary form during the course of the *Paris Review* interview,[13] and the third appeared in the later volume of collected poems, *Reality Sandwiches.* "Psalm I" might be considered a prolegomena to these later poems, as well as to a whole spectrum of quasi-religious verse which began experimentally but which later developed into Ginsberg's primary poetic form. The style of the poem adapts to scriptural form by slackening from the tighter, more sparse type of verse seen in "To-nite all is well." The principle of cleavage between mind and body is continued by means of a contrast in the first line between "vision haunted mind" and "reason which never changes." Oddly enough, the reason and the mind are opposites; a split in the mental process pits vision and spirit against the static, quantitative *modus operandi* of logic. Reason is the language of science—cold and uninspired; but "Mind," haunted, is the poet's openness to a supra-realm beyond the rigidity of cause and effect. Ginsberg's suspicion of the human reason is not based, therefore, upon a belief that man is a poor logician but on the profounder conviction that man is "something more than the best logician." [14]

The words that Ginsberg uses to suggest the supra-logical dimension of the human mind are "gaps" and "flaws." "Gaps" and "flaws" are simply chinks in men's rational armor through which they can make tentative forays into seemingly endless planes of non-rational reality. "My mind," he says in this poem, "is the focus of much lightening," but what he means by "mind" is clearly not the ordinary denotation assigned to the term. "Mind" is not a mere receptor of knowledge but a focal point for visionary insight, and he seems to be deliberately insisting upon a distinction between the "mind" of line two and the "I" which opens line three. "I" is an ego of a lower cause-and-effect plane; it is subject to the vagaries of mood and meteorology. "I" am tired, the poet is saying; and so "I" can't think well today—a simple logical inference. But this "I," this rational ego, Ginsberg seems so eager to point out, is unreliable and has nothing to do with that part of man which is above logical categories. This higher and more authentic nature of man finds syllogisms irrelevant and receives its knowledge of reality through the cracks in the imprisoning walls of logic. "Majestic flaws of the mind" are just that—majestic. They are portals to holiness.

The novelty of this conception for Ginsberg is reflected in the next line where he suggests that his previous work has not followed this inspiration. It has been derivative until now: "an imitation of the literary cackle in my head." "Psalm I," however, is of a new order. It is "gossip," yes, but gossip of a man's nocturnal trysts with reality, which will mean little to readers until they too come to understand that man is something more than the best logician "when the Dove descends." Both the prophet and the egotist appear to haunt these lines, but so too does the spirit of a man who is convinced he has grasped something timeless. "The thing I understood from Blake," Ginsberg explains, "was that it is possible to transmit a message through time which could reach the enlightened, that poetry had a definite effect, it wasn't just pretty, or just beautiful, as I had understood pretty beauty before —it was something basic to human existence, or it reached something, it reached the bottom of human existence." [15]

III *Cézanne*

"Cézanne's Ports" (10) was undoubtedly written with the intention of exciting its readers' "majestic flaws of mind." Although it seems to owe something to William Carlos Williams' much-anthologized "The Yachts," the poem reflects Ginsberg's fascination with Cézanne's attempts to trick the mind out of its customary patterns of reception. What Cézanne hoped to achieve with plastic, visual effects, Ginsberg aspired to accomplish with words. According to Cézanne, the technique was to discover or recover what he termed "*petites sensations*." Paul Tillich, also an admirer of Cézanne's canvases, has described the procedure as an artistic treatment of unorganic cubic forms in such a way that "the power of being itself" becomes embodied in them. It is, he continues, "nothing else than an attempt to look into the depths of reality, below any surface and any beautification of the surface and any organic unity." [16]

Ginsberg's "majestic flaws of mind" (or what he in some cases calls "gaps") are equivalents of *petites sensations* and indeed are intended to be glimpses "into the depths of reality." Close study of the two-dimensional surfaces of Cézanne's paintings, Ginsberg discovered, caused them to flash into three-dimensional space objects.[17] As he squinted at the pictures, three-dimensional "openings" occurred, which were not unlike the cosmic sensations he had experienced in the Blake visions. When he experimented with the phenomenon under the influence of marijuana, he came to the conclusion that Cézanne was actually reconstituting not physical objects into Cubist forms, but rather his own ocular *impressions* of those forms. Cézanne was, in effect, observing his eyeballs observing a scene. Ginsberg suddenly realized that the artist's focus of attention was not outward, toward the object, but inward, toward the *impression* that the object had made upon his consciousness. It was, in fact, an Existential posture; reality was not objective nature "out there," but subjective experience that was lived through by a sentient human being.

The acknowledgment of Reality as an inward experience apprehended through *petites sensations,* or "majestic flaws of mind," is crucial to Ginsberg's conviction of the holiness of everything. "Majestic flaws" are flashes of supra-rational understanding or, as Cézanne has confidently proclaimed, "nothing other than *pater omnipotens aeterna deus.*" [18] The congeniality of this position to Tillich's theological assertion that "faith is the state of being ultimately concerned" [19] is quite evident, and it is also interesting to observe how close Ginsberg's anti-rationalistic position stands to Tillich's further conviction that "we must deny that man's essential nature is identical with the rational character of his mind. Man is able to decide for or against reason, he is able to create beyond reason or to destroy below reason." [20]

The artist's obligation within this context is to create situations where the *pater omnipotens aeterna deus* can speak. The poet or painter must cause breaks in the rational continuity of existence through the uncovering of "flaws" which in turn produce *petites sensations.* In painting, *petites sensations* are achieved through striking placements of geometric masses; in poetry, the masses are supplanted by word images which are juxtaposed to produce flashes of esthetic or godly brilliance. Ginsberg has said that "one can see through his [Cézanne's] canvas to God." [21] The implicit suggestion is that his own poems are equally efficient media.

As a poem, "Cézanne's Ports" pales before the grandiose theory behind it. The cosmic allegory seems painfully strained, particularly so when one considers that it was taken secondhand from the painting; for example: "In the foreground we see time and life swept in a race," and "the other side of the bay/is Heaven and Eternity." Part of Ginsberg's appreciation of this particular painting can be explained by the Oriental esthetic that seems to govern it. The painting (and therefore the poem) centers on what is *not* included within the frame. Ginsberg, for instance, is impressed with the fact that the "meeting place" of the shores (Heaven,

Eternity) "doesn't occur on the canvas" and that there is "a bleak white haze over its mountains." Such interest in the non-represented is all patently mystical, but one feels that looking through this particular glass darkly makes for a smudgy poetic experience.

IV *The Quest for Reality*

"After All, What Else is There to Say" (11) attempts much less than "Cézanne's Ports." This poem about the writing of poetry, implies the question: What is the function of poetry? The answer in the last line is "telling the truth." Between the question and the answer runs one word of pungent, practical advice from Ginsberg on how to achieve the truth: "Wait." Waiting is the writer's strategy for breaking through the veil in order to see the "universe itself." The veil, in this case, is the poet's own mind which "turns/in a kind of feminine madness of chatter." Chatter, like radio static which interferes with communication, is the same thing as "the literary cackle in my head" mentioned in "Psalm I" (9). "Chatter" and "cackle" are obstacles to "telling the truth" because they are the residue of secondhand ideas which clog the channels of pure inspiration. The only way to clear these channels is through sheer patience—waiting. The poet must wait until the scratchy static of his impure immediate response subsides before the scene can speak for itself—before "the sky/appears as it is."

In terms of poetic theory, "After All, What Else is There to Say" is a case study of how Charles Olson's principle ("FORM IS NEVER MORE THAN AN EXTENSION OF CONTENT") is actually put to work. "Chatter" and "cackle" are symptoms of a subversive attempt on the part of the poet's fatal impulse to impose an outside order upon his material. The impulse must be allowed to die before the poem can come into being with fidelity. In other words, the creative issue involves the distinction between rendering and telling a poem. Since Ginsberg at this stage is still strongly influenced by Williams, he clearly feels that rendering is the proper poetic tactic, and so he says,

> I wait . . .
> wait for the moment when
> the poem itself

is my way of speaking out, not
declaiming of celebrating, yet,
but telling the truth.

The title of the poem provides the text against which the description of the creative problem is held in evidence. There *is* nothing else to say, save "*what is in front of* . . . [the poet's] *senses at the moment of writing.*" William Burroughs, the articulator of this conviction, mirrors Ginsberg's position precisely by adding that, as a poet, "I am a recording instrument . . . I do not presume to impose 'story' 'plot' 'continuity' . . ." [22]

Ginsberg's "Fyodor" (11) is an interesting exercise in the subtleties of naming. The names one uses for objects and people have often been used as indices to the relationships one feels toward them, and Ginsberg exploits this human propensity with technical brilliance in this short account of his impressions of Dostoyevsky. Whatever profundity is to be found in this poem is contained in its implicit insistence that the "reality" of Fyodor is not inherent in the Russian novelist himself but lies in the *impressions* of Dostoyevsky that exist in Ginsberg's growing consciousness of the man. One is reminded of Ginsberg's interest in Cézanne in whose work he thought to be witnessing the work of an artist who observed his eyeballs observing a scene.

The various names Ginsberg uses for his Russian subject are the technical media through which he communicates the "reality" of Fyodor at various stages of his experience of him. The first impression, for example, is one of unfamiliarity: "My original version of D./before I read him. . . ." This powerful but as yet unfamiliar acquaintance is characterized by the empty, inconclusive abbreviation "D." Later Fyodor seems to peer into Ginsberg's consciousness with the mystic imprecision of awe: "The death's head of realism," "the dark/haunted-house man, wild, aged,/spectral Russian." When Fyodor becomes an imposing force—mysterious and alien—this impression is reflected in the alien spelling of his name: "Dostoievski." Eventually, Fyodor is read and understood: "realities" coincide, and it is discovered that they are brothers under the skin. "I call him Dusty now," Ginsberg says with American camaraderie, although he acknowledges his lack of exclusive franchise by adding: "but he is Dostoyevsky [American spelling]." The personal illumination of the poem is the poet's admiration of his own prophetic talent even as a child. It is as if to say, "I just knew I'd like Dostoievski even though I've barely heard of him."

V *Rendering versus Telling*

Very often in what is called Emblem poetry a physical description is rendered which is wrenched into significance by a seemingly unrelated title. George Herbert's "The Pulley" is a good example, or one could choose from a myriad of possibilities in the poems of William Carlos Williams. This technique is often associated with paintings in which the artist demands that the viewer "not accept the surface alone" but penetrate "into those depths in which the tension of the forces creates nature." [23] In poetry, the title often serves as a trap door through which the reader plummets to a deeper understanding of what is inherent in the picture rendered for him. One of Ginsberg's early experiments with this technique is "The Trembling of the Veil" (12) which once again exhibits the influence of Dr. Williams.

Two instances in this ostensibly simple, natural, descriptive poem show Ginsberg's deviation from the classic methodology of Williams and point to a characteristic problem in much of Ginsberg's verse. Both instances are similes: (1) the trees "like live organisms on the moon," and (2) the bough "like a hairy protuberance." If one agrees that, in principle, the "rendering" of a poem attempts to avoid metaphor and simile (following Williams' credo of "no ideas but in things"), the meaning of the poem should emerge from its structure and not from some heavy-handed authorial intrusion. It is difficult to defend the similes in this poem, however, because they draw attention *away from* the immediacy of the structural scene. In fact, the similes weaken the climactic *petite sensation* by disclosing it in advance. The similes, in other words, are leaks through which the kinetic energy of the poem prematurely drains. What is the purpose of seeing the trees as lunar "organisms" when the structure of the poem depends upon the reader's acknowledgment that they are distinctively *natural* phenomena? Why must the bough be "hairy" (introducing a confusion between flora and fauna) when it is precisely the botanical essence of the tree that the structural energy of the poem requires?

Nature has been traditionally presented in poetry as a veil which only partially conceals an eternal force behind it. Appropriately, the wind, as a natural force, suggests this universal power by pushing the boughs of the trees downward. The natural phenomena are completely sufficient for the functioning of the poem. "After all," Ginsberg should have said to himself, "What Else is There to Say?" The problem was well put by Robert Hazel when he reviewed *Empty Mirror* for *The Nation:* "These early poems are a development of the anti-poetic principle of Williams, but Ginsberg is not subservient to Williams; he does not, like Williams, carefully keep the voice down, but to a considerable degree restores elements of Cranian rhetoric to the Williams canon." [24] Perhaps an even better diagnosis is Ginsberg's own:

> I attempted to concentrate
> the total sun's rays in
> each poem as through a glass,
> but such magnification
> did not set the page on fire. (18)

In one poem of *Empty Mirror,* "The Bricklayer's Lunch Hour," which is strikingly similar to "The Trembling of the Veil" in form and intention, Ginsberg does "carefully keep the voice down"; and the absence of rhetoric does much toward fulfilling Dr. Williams' counsel that "the writing cannot be made to be 'a kind of prose,' not prose with a dirty wash of a stale poem over it" and also that "it must not set out, as poets are taught or have a tendency to do, to deceive, to sneak over a poetic way of laying down phrases" (6).

Barely qualifying as a vignette, the poem structurally matches the commonplaceness of the scene with a spare, matter-of-fact treatment. The language is good, unsmeared American idiom: unpretentious and carefully calculated to catch the monotony of an unexceptional workday. The effect of the poem depends upon "framing" the inconsequential in order to expose an inherent significance which would otherwise be lost outside the poetic medium. The framing is accomplished by the trivial but essentially human gesture of the laborer placing his hat over a kitten's body, coupled with suggestions of imminent catastrophe: the darkening of the sky and the sudden, harsh wind. The trick of this poem is the way in which Ginsberg has managed to pull something universal out of ordinary workaday trivia. The planned intrusion of universal insight operating in this poem raises the reader's level of consciousness above mere narrative and description. The technique is a slight variation of the "trap-door" technique of tricking the reader into a deeper reality than he had anticipated. The "diamond in the rough" is unexpectedly illuminated; the ordinary is seen to be special.

VI *God and Death*

When Ginsberg experienced his Blake vision in a New York tenement, he crawled out on a fire escape and rapped on the window of a neighboring apartment and screamed, "I have seen God!" [25] He often refers to God in his poetry, but the precise character of his deity is usually clouded in ambiguity. While at times Ginsberg's God is spoken of in transcendent terms, the general impression one gets from the poetry is that "God" is an imminent kind of depth-dimension who is accessible through vision, love, introspection, and hallucination. God's residence is definitely in this world, and His presence is unlimited: "The world is holy! . . . Everyman's an angel!" (*Howl*, 2).

Despite the lurid descriptions and drawings of "The Great Being" that Ginsberg recalls from his experimentation with the powerful drug, *yage*, his day-to-day theological persuasions reflect the unrest and concern that most conscientious people feel today. In short, Ginsberg has been "Honest to God" in the sense that Bishop Robinson has repopularized the phrase by admitting Him into the fabric of the world. It might be concluded that this view, while it does not pronounce the last rites on the Almighty, does inter Him in the worldly existence of men. Heaven is obsolete; "The shrouded Stranger" has taken up new residence "upon the city dump" (46).

Rejection of Heaven compels acceptance of finite Earth. Camus has said, "This hell of the present is . . . [man's] Kingdom at last," [26] and Walt Whitman has declared, "I accept Time absolutely." [27] Allen Ginsberg follows them in a short poem called "Metaphysics" (15):

> This is the one and only
> firmament . . .

There is no other world.
. . . .
I am living in Eternity.

The equation could not be simpler: the world equals eternity; worldly existence is the only one human beings will ever know.

Such a view requires serious consideration of the significance of Death, and Ginsberg provides three poems in this *Empty Mirror* which meet the issue directly. The first, "In Death, Cannot Reach What is Most Near" (15), is the most complex. The poem opens with what appears to be a conundrum:

We know all about death that
we will ever know because
we have all experienced
the state before birth.

Because there is no cognition before birth, it seems clear that one can know nothing of death. Death becomes a shadowy, ineffable blackness which frames human existence. Men are imprisoned in their finitude, and Ginsberg continues the pursuit of this idea by an allusion to the Venerable Bede's famous metaphor:

Life seems a passage between
two doors to the darkness.
Both are the same and truly
eternal and perhaps it may
be said that we meet in
darkness. The nature of time
is illuminated by this
meeting of eternal ends.

That the "nature of time" should be "illuminated" by the blackness of Eternity on either side of human life is an Existential concept which Norman Mailer has exploited in order to propound his conviction that living with death should encourage one to cultivate his "psychopathic brilliance." [28] Eternity, in other words, is a black mystery which encloses man's life span and which forces him to focus all his attention on his being rather than on some afterlife.

"In Death, Cannot Reach What is Most Near" contains essentially the same philosophy as "Metaphysics"; both poems express an Existential allegiance to the here and the now. Nevertheless, the problem of Death itself is still not satisfactorily clarified; it is treated enigmatically:

> It is amazing to think that
> thought and personality
> of man is perpetuated in
> time after his passage
> to eternity. And one time
> is all Time if you look
> at it out of the grave. (15)

What is the reader to make of this assertion? The first five lines offer little difficulty; they simply echo an Elizabethan trust in Art as a form of immortality: a poet's verses, for example, live on after his demise. But the conclusion of Ginsberg's poem is not quite so simple because of the introduction of the time paradox. "One time" and "all Time" appear as two separate concepts which become reconciled only in "the grave." "One time" clearly means one man's life span; accordingly, "all Time" must refer to Eternity. A passage from Whitman's "Song of Myself" seems relevant here: ". . . I accept Time absolutely./It alone is without flaw, it alone rounds and completes all,/That mystic baffling wonder alone completes all." [29]

The time that Whitman talks about seems the same as Ginsberg's "all Time." "All Time" is the eternal blackness which defines the limits of human life span and which is necessarily a "mystic baffling wonder." The fact that "all Time" and "one time" become the same from the viewpoint of the grave assures one that an honest acknowledgment of Death is also an honest acceptance of Life. Whitman's declaration ("I accept Time absolutely") is an honest denial of immortality which Ginsberg appears to share. One should not delude himself by understanding death as a "vague possibility" or a "remote horizon";[30] he should accept it as the end of being. He must, along with the poet Rilke, have "the ability to read the word death without a negative response." [31] He must live with death as a constant companion—even as a friend.

The second poem, "This is About Death" (16), obliquely follows the same theme. The word "Death" appears only in the title, for the poem speaks of only "Art" and "Being," and the reader is required to make the necessary connections. The function of Art is to remind forgetful people that "Being is the one thing/all the universe shouts." This is also the message of "Metaphysics" and "In Death, Cannot Reach What is Near." Obviously, the coherence of "This is About Death" depends upon a relationship between Being and Death, and such a relationship seems to have been implicitly drawn in the prior poems. The essence seems to be that Being *requires* freedom toward death, for fear of death takes one away from Being—and hence from reality—and it also encourages a narcotic dependence upon myths such as the ones so brilliantly satirized in Evelyn Waugh's *The Loved One*. A more mature stance toward death is co-existence, and this posture seemingly is that of the Existentialist and the "hipster" alike. "If the fate of twentieth century man is to live with death from adolescence to premature senescence," writes Norman Mailer, "why then the only life-giving answer is to accept the terms of death, to live with death as immediate danger, to divorce oneself from society, to exist without roots, to set out on that uncharted journey into the rebellious imperatives of the self." [32]

Some of the perils of Mailer's "life-giving answer" are catalogued in the third of Ginsberg's death poems, "I have Increased Power" (23–24). Whatever salutary effects come from an honest facing of death, there is the knowledge that "reality can be Joy or terror" (24) and that one who lives must continually face "the grimness of chance." Certainly, the grim chanciness of life could not be more luridly expressed than in the last lines of this poem:

> How often have I
> had occasion to see
> existence display
> the affections
> of a bloodthirsty
> negro homosexual.

VII *Reality and Dream Allegories*

"The Terms in Which I Think of Reality" (28–29) is a tripartite sociophilosophical sounding of Ginsberg's dialogue with the world. The first stanza rather neatly links this effort with the three previous ventures into philosophy with an insistence upon the finiteness of man's ontological predicament:

> Reality is a question
> of realizing how real
> the world is already.

The stanza promises a program of a demythologization and carries through with a series of premises already implied in the previous poems: "Time is Eternity," "everyone's an angel," and the like. The equation of Time with Eternity is a paradoxical assertion which supplants objective time-*keeping* with subjective time-*living*. The according of angelic status to all men is not flattery but a hopeful conviction that men are indeed angels under their thick skins of hypocrisy. The new element introduced in this poem is the idea that reality is "Heaven's mystery/of changing perfection." Eternity (which is Time) is not an absolute; in fact, "absolutely Eternity/changes!" Evidence? "Cars are always/going down the street,/lamps go off and on." Man lives in Eternity. Eternity is real. Reality changes.

All that is left to complete this first section is a moral judgment, and it comes in esthetic clothing: "The motion/of change is beautiful, as well as form called/in and out of being." Change (death being the supreme mutation) is nature's secret source of beauty, and the first part of the poem ends on that note. As a statement of position, this section perhaps suffices. As poetry, however, it is not much more than a metaphysician's hasty outline of Wallace Stevens' "Sunday Morning." Ginsberg is clearly out of his metiér.

Phase two of "The Terms in Which I Think of Reality" is putting theory into practice or, as Ginsberg rather verbosely puts it,

> . . . to distinguish process
> in its particularity with
> an eye to the initiation
>
> of gratifying new changes
> desired in the real world. (29)

This language is simply indefensible as prose, poetry, or even satire. If one refers to Wallace Stevens again for a moment, one can see in that poet a man capable of poking fun at pedagoguery:

> Nota: man is the intelligence of his soul,
> The sovereign ghost. As such, the Socrates
> Of snails, musician of pears, principium
> And Lex.[33]

Ginsberg is *not* poking fun; or, if he is, he has no talent for it. Neither is he speaking (as Williams claims in the Introduction that he should) "in plain terms, such as men will recognize" (5–6). The intent here is not to compare Ginsberg to Stevens, but merely to point out that Ginsberg has allowed himself to become derailed from his natural track.[34] What he wants to say is simply that the present world is full of unpleasantness, and the only way one can improve it is by bits and pieces. The practical movement of the poet's intention is blunted and deformed by a sophomoric pseudo-rhetoric.

Part three of the poem abandons the previous method and deals with the universal situation of man in a less-than-perfect world. The medium is an extended metaphor in which man is likened to "the unhappy/whore on River Street," and his sad plight is unraveled in the idiom of prostitution. Thus, the oldest dilemma in the world is presented in terms of the oldest profession. The search for love is rewarded with "snide remarks" and "a couple of bucks." Even worse, the poor whore, man, has "never really heard of a glad/job or joyous marriage or/a difference in the heart:/or thinks it isn't for her,/which is her worst misery." The theorized reality of part *a* is unknown to the factual reality of part *c*. The chasm that separates the two constitutes the greatest tragedy of all.

Scattered throughout *Empty Mirror* are poems that fall roughly under the heading of dream allegories. They are all narrative in structure, and they generally center on some aspect of social sickness that Ginsberg usually sees in terms of a man thrown into a Kafkaesque situation of meaninglessness and finding no way nor no one with whom to communicate. "A Crazy Spiritual" is one example; "Two Boys went into a Dream Diner," another. Some have a semi-humorous yet ironic twist to them such as "How Come He Got Canned at the Ribbon Factory" or "The Archtype Poem." Typical of this kind of poem is "A Meaningless Institution" (13).

The "enormous ward" in which the protagonist of the poem is

thrust is a form of dramatization of the Ginsberg-Heidegger analysis of existence in which man is called upon to acknowledge his ignorance of his "whence and wither" and to skirmish as best he can in an apparently irrational world. The ward is deliberately reminiscent of a military barracks, and the narrator is issued "bedding, and a bunk . . . surrounded by hundreds of weeping,/decaying men and women." From a vantage point "three tiers up," he enjoys an overview of the world—similar to scenes from *Piers Plowman*—which reveals "grey aisles," "Old, crippled, dumb people," and "a heavy girl/in a dirty dress" who stares at him. The feeling of paralysis that the description engenders seems to derive from a total absence of communication. There is no one to explain, no one to advise. He waits, incommunicado "for an official guide to come/and give me instructions"; but, of course, there is none. The denouement is the archetype catastrophe of meaninglessness:

> After awhile, I wandered
> off down empty corridors
> in search of a toilet.

This theme, perhaps, is the classic one of the twentieth century. Ginsberg's forlorn hero, just another confused mute "waiting for Godot," finally gives up his senseless vigil for a cosmic guide and attends to the practical necessities of animal nature. The moral is suggestively anchored in the title: "A Meaningless Institution." The two nouns irrevocably correspond; all institutions are meaningless, and the human tragedy is that man has forfeited his birthright by institutionalizing his existence.

Is there any way out of such a predicament? One exit sign flickers dimly in the poem "In Society" (14). In this "dream," written a year before "A Meaningless Institution," one finds an almost identical form and theme; only the scene has been changed. The poem moves from a ward to a cocktail party. Toward the end of the poem, the narrator is rebuffed by a "fluffy female who looked like/a princess." She glares at the hero and says, "I don't like you," and turns her head away, refusing to be introduced. The allegory is fairly explicit: it is a case of perverse refusal to communicate with an implicit suggestion that the "princess" has forgotten (or never known) that she is really an "angel." "How/can you decide when you don't even/know me," the hero rages; and then, as if to shout his presence into the room—to communicate in the only way possible in an incommunicable world—the narrator says:

> I continued in a violent
> and messianic voice, inspired at
> last, dominating the whole room.

The "messianic voice," which is to become Ginsberg's hallmark in later poetry, perhaps finds its justification in this poem. In a world that doesn't listen, in one that is a "narcissistic bitch," the poet's only recourse is not merely to shout but to howl. Eight years later Ginsberg carries this tactic to its extreme.

Some of the best poetry in *Empty Mirror* is the least pretentious and the most indebted to William Carlos Williams if for no other reason than it deals with "the literal *things* of an immediate environment." These poems require no explanation, only acknowledgment and appreciation; for they are pure communication in the best poetical sense of the word. They include such verses as "Sunset" (26) with its opening lines: "The whole blear world/of smoke and twisted steel/around my head in a railroad/car . . ." or "A Ghost May Come" (26) with its simple haunting catalogue of objects on a table. In these poems is the sound of "the shuffling of human beings in all the stages of their day" (5).

On the other hand, there are also the grand flights. Not the "grand flights" of Wallace Stevens which are "one's Sunday baths,/One's tootings at the weddings of the soul" which "Occur as they occur." [35] Ginsberg's grand flights do *not* simply "occur"; they are strenuously induced. Too often there is a tedious straining for profundity such as in the final piece of this volume "The Shrouded Stranger," a phrase of which provides the title for the collection. The poem begins boldly and alliteratively: "The Shroudy Stranger's reft of realms./Abhorred he sits upon the city dump./His broken heart's a bag of shit./The vast rainfall, an empty mirror" (46–47).

The poem is mystical, haunting, and Existential, despite its over-Romantic machinery; but even Ginsberg, by the time he gets to the fourth section, begins to see the futility. "It was to have a structure," he apologizes, "it/was going to tell a story;/it was to be a mass of images/moving on a page, with/a hollow voice at the center." In too many of Ginsberg's grand flights, a hollow voice appears in the center where more heart ought to be. Poetry does not live on rhetoric alone, and this is one of the problems one must continually consider in Ginsberg's work.

VIII *Previews of Coming Attractions*

Of all the poems in *Empty Mirror,* three in particular provide the most reliable preview of coming attractions: "Psalm I," "Hymn," and "Paterson." All three represent quests for what might be called a "hip" version of the Beatific Vision, and it is not accidental that they should all avail themselves of essentially religious (and particularly Christian) symbology and form. "Psalm I," which has already been discussed, sets the pattern for the other two with its insistence upon a separation between "the vision haunted Mind" and "that reason which never changes" (9). The poem plots the direction by placing absolute trust in "the majestic flaws of mind," and it introduces the prophetic theme by implying that "this gossip" will be "lost in a library and rediscovered when the Dove descends." The analogy of the process to the phenomenon of Christian faith is irresistible: the "natural man" of "flesh and blood" turns his thoughts away from things of the world, he experiences a faith in something beyond himself through "evidence of things unseen," and he awaits the second coming of Christ when "the Dove descends."

In "Hymn" (25), the form continues its religious character; but the "messianic voice" is given free rein. The result is a mystic quality which echoes the baroque excesses of the seventeenth-century Richard Crashaw or even Christopher Smart, who is, according to Ginsberg, a seminal influence on his later form.[36] The first "line" of this poem, which is better described as a superlyrical "take-off" (Ginsberg calls these outbursts "gone dithyrambs"),[37] expresses the need for a unique poetic form to deal with his unique subject matter: "No hyacinthe imagination can express this clock of meat bleakly pining for its sweet immaterial paradise. . . ." The "clock of meat" is, in religious terms, the natural, "unregenerate man" who is still shackled by a chronological understanding of his existence instead of by a Bergsonian appreciation of human life. The problem posed is the metamorphosis of the "clock of meat" into the "clock of light" which is "the very summa and dove of the unshrounding [*sic*] of finality's joy. . . ." Again, this process is best understood in relation to Christian regeneration.

The poem continues in an increasingly ecstatic pitch, like angels ascending "stoops of light up the celestial fire escape" in anticipation of "when the final gate is opened and the Diamond Seraph . . . asks us in the Name of the Lord to share that Love in Heaven which on Earth was so disinherited." The passionate aspiration for mystic vision—the divine lust to share in heavenly Love "which on Earth was so disinherited"—underscores an extreme disillusionment with the world as it is, which in turn is coupled with a desperate trust in the existence of the ideal.

The mystic "otherworldliness" of this poem clashes with the bulk of other religio-philosophic poems, which causes some confusion in understanding of Ginsberg's precise theological stance. The persistent equation of Time and Eternity, for example, as well as the constant, implicit suggestion that the only Heaven man will find is one which already exists on earth ("Everyman's an angel"), leads one to the conclusion that the religious symbolism in this poem is formal machinery rather than an authentic statement of belief. At the same time, one is reminded of the lament in "I Have Increased My Power" where Ginsberg writes with obvious honesty: "Trouble with/me now, no active life/in realworld" (23).

Perhaps the best explanation is that the confusion of these poems is not a basis for criticism of them but of their subject. Perhaps it is, as Dr. Williams suggests in his Introduction, that "this young Jewish boy, already not so young any more, has recognized something that has escaped most of the modern age, he has found that man is lost in the world of his own head" (5). "Paterson" (39–40), if it is not wholly a portrait of a man "lost in the world of his own head," is at least a shuddering account of a poet making a decision between two possibilities of existence.

Nikolai Berdyaev has written what might have been the perfect prose prelude to Ginsberg's "Paterson":

> The commonplace in life, the repetitions and imitations, the fetters and repressions of life have produced in me a sense of tedium and drawn me into a void of nothingness. . . . The final and infernal limit of tedium is reached when man says to himself that nothing is. Suffering is, no doubt, a relief and a salvation in such

> a human condition, for it is a way of regaining the depth of life. Anguish too may bring salvation. There are people who feel happy in the midst of their own and the world's emptiness, and this state may well be the supreme instance of triviality and the commonplace.[38]

The tedium Berdyaev speaks of is wonderfully mirrored in the first half of Ginsberg's poem: "What do I want in these rooms papered with visions of money?" the poet asks. "How much can I make by cutting my hair? If I put new heels on my shoes,/bathe my body reeking of masturbation and sweat, layer upon layer of excrement/dried in employment bureaus, magazine hallways, statistical cubicles, factory stairways . . . ?" The metaphor is wages, and the age-old question of "what does it profit a man . . ." is swept into modern idiom. "What war I enter and for what prize!" Ginsberg wearily exclaims; and the answer is readily at hand: "the dead prick of commonplace obsession,/harridan vision of electricity at night and daylight misery of thumbsucking rage" (39).

Not only is Berdyaev's "tedium" very much present in these lines, but also his "anguish" which "too may bring salvation." The second half of the poem presents an Existential "salvation" to which Berdyaev has given the name "suffering." Suffering "is a way of regaining the depth of life" which Ginsberg seems instinctively to realize by defiantly choosing the Beat way of life:

> I would rather go mad, gone down the dark road to Mexico,
> heroin dripping in my veins,
> eyes and ears full of marijuana,
> eating the god Peyote on the floor of a mudhut on the border
> or laying in a hotel room over the body of some suffering man
> or woman. (39)

Ginsberg has of course done all these things—the program of anguish becomes autobiography—but for poetical purposes the catalogue of alternatives to the tedious "reality of wrath," from which he finds it imperative to escape, is engineered to inflame every moral fiber of the presumptuous "department store supervisory employees" from whom this poem is a Declaration of Independence. The vocabulary—the shock technique—is calculated to frighten: veins dripping with heroin, "ears full of marijuana," "the

God Peyote," and illicit sex (hetero- and homosexual). The "either/or" is painted in the most vivid hues in order to verify the depth of the conviction.

Even more shocking, however, is the way Ginsberg then identifies his lurid preferences with the historical crisis of the Christian faith. It is not a shoddy attempt to usurp a respectable ally; it is a genuine declaration that his program is identical to Christ's! Both travel a road leading to salvation; both strive to regain the "depth of life." Says Ginsberg:

> [I would] rather drag a rotten railroad tie to a Golgotha in the
> Rockies;
> rather, crowded with thorns in Galveston, nailed hand and foot
> in Los Angeles, raised up to die in Denver,
> pierced in the side in Chicago, perished and tombed in New
> Orleans and resurrected in 1958 somewhere on
> Garret Mountain,
> come down soaring in a blaze of hot cars and garbage. . . . (39)

Ginsberg would like to be a modern Christ; and, things being the way they are, his reconstruction of Christ's activity in the twentieth century has the same arresting shock value that it had two thousand years ago. While looking for the Shrouded Stranger, Ginsberg finally "met him face to face at last," and "didn't even recognize him": " 'I'll bet you didn't think/it was me after all,' he said" (47). Too often Ginsberg's temptation is to consider this conversation self-dialogue.

As the title page relates, *Empty Mirror* is a collection of Allen Ginsberg's early poems; but it might be wise to add also the adjective "transitional." The volume gives a fairly clear picture of where Ginsberg's poetry is going; but, at the same time, it is full of examples of where it has been. The technical control and concern over precise form that one sees in the front of the book are certainly indications of Ginsberg's immense debt to the late William Carlos Williams. As one moves further and further into *Empty Mirror,* however, one sees the Williams influence giving way to an impassioned, uninhibited style which eventually erupts in *Howl*—the subject of the next chapter.

CHAPTER 4

Howl and Other Poems

I *History of* Howl

DESPITE the fact that it has been fashionable to say that *Howl* exploded on the American literary scene like a bombshell, that San Francisco finally "turned Ginsberg on," and that this poem heralded in the Beat Generation, it is difficult to find in this admittedly extraordinary poem much that has not been anticipated in inchoate and sometimes even mature form in *Empty Mirror*. *Howl* is perhaps a crystallization of many incipient attitudes and techniques that had been residing in Ginsberg for years, but it is hardly the beginning of a new poetic direction or even a sudden eruption of outrage. It cannot even be said that *Howl* is necessarily uniquely modern in form or intention. Most would have to agree with Kenneth Rexroth that this type of poetry is "in one of the oldest traditions, that of Hosea or the other, angry Minor Prophets of the Bible." [1] *Howl*, therefore, is not a genesis; it is an amplification.

Part of the reason for considering *Howl* an amplification has nothing to do with literature at all. The furor surrounding its initial publication was like a shot heard round the world. The poem was immediately enshrouded by so much sensationalism during the months of litigation which followed its release that there was little opportunity for much sober, reflective digestion of the poem to have occurred. The press, with its appetite whetted for sensationalism rather than for impartial assessment, had a field day. Responsible commentary appeared mostly in Judge Horn's courtroom where the atmosphere was at least as much political as literary. As an example of the complete critical inadequacy with which the poem was first received, Lawrence Ferlinghetti—commenting on testimony made by a prosecution witness (an instructor from the Catholic University of San Francisco) who had remarked: "You feel like you are going through the gutter when you have to read that stuff"—observed that "the critically devastating things the prosecution's witnesses could have said, but didn't, remain one of the great Catholic silences of the day." [2] If nothing else, the legal proceedings brought against *Howl* for obscenity served to make it easily one of the best-selling volumes of poetry of the twentieth century.

Howl was published by Ferlinghetti's City Lights Books in San Francisco as a part of the Pocket Poets Series. The first edition was printed in England by Villiers, passed through United States Customs, and was subsequently delivered to San Francisco for publication in the fall of 1956. A series of almost comical legal interventions then led to the ultimate "obscenity" trial which eventually pronounced *Howl and Other Poems* as *not* being without "the slightest redeeming social importance." In other words, in the eyes of the court, it was found not to be obscene.

The first event leading to the trial occurred on March 24, 1957, when a portion of a second printing of the volume was stopped by custom officials on the basis of Section 305 of the Tariff Act of 1930. The San Francisco *Chronicle* quoted Chester MacPhee, the collector of customs, as saying that "the words and the sense of the writing is obscene. You wouldn't want your children to come across it." [3] Shortly afterward, the American Civil Liberties Union objected to the action after having read the manuscript supplied to it by the publisher, Mr. Ferlinghetti. While this litigation was going on, a new edition of *Howl* was being printed in the United States which took it out of the jurisdiction of Customs.

A little over a month later, Ferlinghetti published an article in the San Francisco *Chronicle* in which, as he himself paraphrases, "I recommended a medal be made for Collector MacPhee, since his action was already rendering the book famous. But the police were soon to take over this advertising account and do a much better job—10,000 copies of *Howl* were in print by the time they finished with it." In a more serious vein, Ferlinghetti went on to say, "It is not the poet but what he observes which is revealed as obscene. The great obscene wastes of *Howl* are the sad wastes of the mechanized world, lost among atom bombs and insane nationalisms." [4]

The stand of the customs officials crumbled shortly afterward when the United States attorney in San Francisco refused to act against *Howl:* the books were released. But this was only an interlude. Within a week, Ferlinghetti was arrested by a representative of the juvenile department ("Well named, in this case," Ferlinghetti wryly remarks[5]) of the San Francisco police department. The American Civil Liberties Union posted bail, but the fight had started.

Ferlinghetti has documented a representative selection of critical support for *Howl* in his article "Horn on *Howl,*" which has been published in the *Evergreen Review.*[6] A few random excerpts provide some appreciation of a rare situation in which a literary production has received unqualified praise, demonstrating, perhaps, the superiority of righteous indignation raised in the defense of one's own to dull critical swords: ". . . I only wish to say that the book is a thoroughly serious work of literary art" (Henry Rago, editor of *Poetry*); "*Howl and Other Poems* . . . is a dignified, sincere and admirable work of art . . ." (William Hogan of the San Francisco *Chronicle*); "The poet [Ginsberg] gives us the most painful details; he moves us toward a statement of experience that is challenging and finally noble" (Robert Duncan and Director Ruth Witt-Diamant of the San Francisco Poetry Center); ". . . *Howl* is one of the most important books of poetry published in the last ten years" (Thomas Parkinson); ". . . the book has considerable distinction as literature, being a powerful and artistic expression of a meaningful philosophical attitude . . ." (James Laughlin of *New Directions*).[7]

In the course of the trial, numerous witnesses for the defense offered more detailed explication of the poet's intent—but with no less lavish praise. Most informative are the testimonies of Professor Mark Shorer of the University of California and of Kenneth Rexroth. The following portion of Professor's Shorer's testimony from the trial transcript was reprinted in Ferlinghetti's *Evergreen Review* article:

> The theme of the poem is announced very clearly in the opening line. . . . Then the following lines that make up the first part attempt to create the impression of a kind of nightmare world in which people representing "the best minds of my generation," in the author's view, are wandering like damned souls in hell. That is done through a kind of series of what one might call surrealistic images, a kind of state of hallucinations. Then in the second section the mood of the poem changes and it becomes an indictment

> of those elements in modern society that, in the author's view, are destructive of the best qualities in human nature and of the best minds. Those elements are, I would say, predominantly materialism, conformity and mechanization leading toward war. And then the third part is a personal address to a friend, real or fictional, of the poet or of the person who is speaking in the poet's voice—those are not always the same thing—who is mad and in a madhouse, and is the specific representative of what the author regards as a general condition. . . .[8]

Shorer provides as good a statement of the structure, theme, and general strategy of the poem as is possible under the circumstances. Kenneth Rexroth adds additional dimension in his testimony by associating *Howl* with biblical tradition and by evincing sophisticated forensic tactics as well as an acute literary perspicuity:

> The simplest term for such writing is prophetic, it is easier to call it that than anything else because we have a large body of prophetic writing to refer to. There are the prophets of the Bible, which it [*Howl*] greatly resembles in purpose and in language and in subject matter. . . . The theme is the denunciation of evil and a pointing out of the way out, so to speak. That is prophetic literature. "Woe! Woe! Woe! The City of Jerusalem! The Syrian is about to come down or has already and you are to do such and such a thing and you must repent and do thus and so." And *Howl,* the four parts of the poem—that is including the "Footnote to *Howl*" as one additional part—do this very specifically. They take up these various specifics seriatim, one after the other. . . . And "Footnote to *Howl,*" of course, again, is Biblical in reference. The reference is to the Benedicite, which says over and over again, "Blessed is the fire, Blessed is the light, Blessed are the trees, and Blessed is this and Blessed is that," and he [Ginsberg] is saying, "Everything that is human is Holy to me," and that the possibility of salvation in this terrible situation which he reveals is through love and through the love of everything Holy in man. So that, I would say, that this just about covers the field of typically prophetic poetry. . . .[9]

This early criticism points out the two decisive features of *Howl* that serve as positive and negative poles for most of Ginsberg's poetry to follow: Existential despair and the implicit optimism of scriptural prophecy. Since the issue of the trial was quickly pared down to the question of *Howl's* social relevance, esthetic considerations quite naturally were held in abeyance.

II *The Poem*

It is probably best to begin the examination of the poem's literary authenticity with Ginsberg's own views, which are quite extensive. There is no question that Ginsberg himself considered the writing of *Howl* to be a new phase in his poetic development—one best characterized as one of total creative freedom. Specifically, this freedom seems mainly to have consisted of an escape from "fear" to complete honesty. "I thought I wouldn't write a *poem*," he explains, "but just write what I wanted to without fear, let my imagination go, open secrecy, and scribble magic lines from my real mind—sum up my life—something I wouldn't be able to show anybody, write for my own soul's ear and a few other golden ears." [10] The source of the fear he speaks of was not official censorship so much as a crippling, almost Freudian, self-censorship. This fear or self-censorship is evident in his remarks in the *Paris Review* interview previously referred to in Chapter 2.

A second aspect of the total creative freedom of the poem is metrical. While, in retrospect, Ginsberg often accommodates the *literati* by attempting to classify his metrical form ("like [in] certain passages of *Howl* and certain passages of *Kaddish*—there are definite rhythms which could be analyzed as corresponding to classical rhythms, though not necessarily *English* classical rhythms, or Sanscrit prosody" [11]), at the moment of creation he insists that he is "working with my own neural impulses and writing impulses." He then explains the technique in a way that suggests the full extent of the sort of metrical freedom *Howl* demonstrates:

> . . . I wasn't really working with a classical unit, I was working with my own neural impulses and writing impulses. See, the difference is between someone sitting down to write a poem *in* a definite preconceived metrical pattern and filling in that pattern, and someone working with his physiological movements and arriving at a pattern, and perhaps even arriving at a pattern which might even have a name, or might even have a classical usage, but arriving at it organically rather than synthetically. Nobody's got

> any objection to even iambic pentameter if it comes from a source deeper than the mind, that is to say if it comes from the breathing and the belly and the lungs.[12]

Ginsberg's description of the circumstances in which he wrote the first section of *Howl* certainly substantiates the "freewheeling" formal stance he avers above. It was "typed out madly in one afternoon, a tragic custard-pie comedy of wild phrasing, meaningless images for the beauty of abstract poetry of mind running along making awkward combinations like Charley Chaplin's walk, long saxophone-like chorus lines I knew Kerouac would hear *sound* of—Taking off from his own inspired prose line really a new poetry." [13]

Homage is paid to a new master in this statement—Jack Kerouac—which once again documents the occurrence in Ginsberg's career of a shift in allegiances. The cautious and modulated declarations of independence of William Carlos Williams have been replaced by the wilder, more Romantic impulses of Kerouac, Christopher Smart, Whitman, biblical rhetoric, and, of course, Blake. It is as if Kerouac had managed to liberate Ginsberg from all writing inhibitions and to set him on a path of Romantic, cathartic expression which eschewed any interference from the mind.

It is quite easy to take a dim view of this Romantic indulgence and to agree with Yvor Winters' observation that "nearly all romantics decry the intellect and philosophy, yet they offer justifications, necessarily incoherent but none the less rational in intention, of their attitude; they are prone to belittle literary technique, yet they write, and too often with small efficiency; they preach, in the main, the doctrine of moral equivalence, yet their very action, whether private or literary, since it rests on a choice, is a denial of the doctrine." [14] The difficult task of talking about *Howl* in terms of literary criticism is certainly demonstrated in this remark; but to refuse to deal with the poetry on its own terms is to stick one's head in the sand next to the ostrich's. At any rate, the phenomenon of *Howl* was not a sudden thing, despite Ginsberg's claim that it was "really a new poetry." [15] As has been noted, he had been doing much the same sort of thing before without the spotlight of public attention upon him. Publicity, not poetic form, was probably the real innovation.

The first part of *Howl* structurally is a list of atrocities that have been committed specifically to Ginsberg himself and to those in his circle of friends. More generally, these atrocities accumulate to form a desperate critique of a civilization that has set up a power structure which determines men's "mode of consciousness . . . sexual enjoyments . . . different labors and . . . loves." [16] The theme is clearly the same as Ginsberg's essay, "Poetry, Violence, and the Trembling Lambs," in which he pleads: "When will we discover an America that will not deny its own God? Who takes up arms, money, police, and a million hands to murder the consciousness of God? Who spits in the beautiful face of Poetry which sings the Glory of God and weeps in the dust of the world?" [17]

This is prose, but it could easily be inserted into the text of *Howl* without change. Even the structural device of the recurring word "who" is exploited, which demonstrates how blurred, even nonexistent, is the line between poetry and prose in Ginsberg's work. The word "who," Ginsberg has explained, was used in *Howl* "to keep the beat, a base to keep measure, return to and take off from again onto another streak of invention." [18] One might even say that "who" was Ginsberg's point of contact between vision and reality—an anchor which regularly brought his free flights back to earth and kept the poem from disappearing into the mists of a subjective wasteland.

"Who," it can be said, also served as an organizational excuse; by its sanction, otherwise unrelated chunks of inspiration could be thrown spontaneously into the poem. In other words, the device was a structural shield which kept "thinking" at bay, thereby allowing imaginative illumination and association unlimited freedom. Ginsberg's reiterative device suggests, of course, the influence of Whitman. As Gay Wilson Allen has pointed out, "Whitman's parallelism, or thought rhythm, is so often accompanied and reinforced by parallel wording and sounds that the two techniques are often almost identical. An easy way to collect examples of Whitman's 'thought rhythm' is to glance down the left-hand margin and notice the lines beginning with the same word, and usually the same grammatical construction: 'I will . . . I will . . . I will . . .' or 'Where . . . Where . . . Where . . .' or 'When . . . When . . . When . . . ,' etc." [19]

Such a technique is indicative of a poetic movement that is cumulative rather than logical or progressive, as Allen also observes; and it becomes uniquely suited to what he calls an "expanding ego psychology." Such a psychology, to follow Allen's argument further, "results in an enumerative style, the cataloging of a representative and symbolical succession of images, conveying the sensation of pantheistic unity and endless becoming." Ginsberg's supreme celebration of "pantheistic unity" is nowhere better sought than in "Footnote to *Howl*." Obviously, the cumulative technique goes back even further to Hebraic roots which Ginsberg also acknowledges as influences upon his work; and Allen goes on to say that "the Hebraic poet developed a rhythm of thought, repeating and balancing ideas and sentences (or independent clauses) instead of syllables or accents." [20]

This criticism of Whitman is relative to *Howl* not only because this poetry exploits the devices of accumulation and parallelism so obviously but also because the unit of this poem is so decisively the line, even when the particular line is attenuated to meet the demands of an inspirational flight. This comment leads us to an interesting point made by E. C. Ross who, while speaking specifically of Whitman's poetry, could also well have been referring to Ginsberg's *Howl*. "Whitman's verse," says Ross, "with the exception that it is not metered—is farther removed from prose than is traditional verse itself, for the reason that the traditional verse is, like prose, composed in sentences, whereas Whitman's verse is composed in lines. . . . A run-on line is rare in Whitman. . . . The law of his structure is that *the unit of sense is the measure of the line*." [21] Precisely the same law of structure holds true for Ginsberg's *Howl* and shows the extent of his debt to Whitman, as well as providing some rationale for regarding *Howl* as poetry.

To read *Howl* properly, then, is to avoid the impulse to search for a logic or a rational connection of ideas. Ginsberg is the first to acknowledge this fact: "the whole first section . . . a tragic custard-pie comedy of wild phrasing and meaningless images. . . ." [22] Therefore, *Howl* must be read the same way Whitman's poetry must be read, but with a twentieth-century consciousness. Ginsberg himself has lamented that "everybody assumes . . . that his [Whitman's] line is a big freakish uncontrollable necessary prosaic goof. No attempt's been made to use it in the light of early XX Century organization of new speech-rhythm prosody to *build up* large organic structures." [23] *Howl* seems to be an experiment along these lines.

The yardsticks to measure the worth of the first part of *Howl* are reduced to basically two: the "tightness" of the catalogue and the maintenance of spontaneity. The first measurement has to do with what Ginsberg would call "density"—the richness of imagery packed into a given line. By and large, the poem does achieve density. Such richness as one finds, however, is achieved at the cost of grammatical continuity; but the same could be said of Whitman. Also, since the movement of the poem is not logical but cumulative, grammatical logic ceases to become a serious concern, and it naturally gives way to sometimes ambiguous, imagistic communication. It is no accident that the entire seventy-eight-line first section counts grammatically as a single sentence.

A substantial portion of the poem's density is also supplied by the method Ginsberg derived from Cézanne's optic tricks—the *petites sensations*. Their verbal equivalents in *Howl* are such juxtapositions as "negro streets," "angry fix," "paint hotels," "blind streets," Peyote solidities," "hydrogen jukebox," and so on endlessly throughout the poem. "I used a lot of [Cézanne's] material in the references in the last part of the first section of *Howl:* 'sensation of Pater Omnipotens Aeterna Deus,'" Ginsberg has said. "The last part of *Howl* was really an homage to art but also in specific terms an homage to Cézanne's method, in a sense I adapted what I could to writing. . . ." [24]

The second measuring stick for evaluating *Howl* is its spontaneity. "But how sustain a long line in poetry (lest it lapse into prosaic)?" [25] Ginsberg has asked himself. A potent answer, as has been observed, is readily available in Charles Olson's principle: "ONE PERCEPTION MUST IMMEDIATELY AND DIRECTLY LEAD TO A FURTHER PERCEPTION." If this declaration can be summarized in one word, it would have to be *speed.* Spontaneity lives on speed, and the creating poet must avoid the lag. He does so, it seems, through association; for many examples of association are operative in the first part of *Howl,* but Ginsberg has himself specifically described how he uses the principle of association in the second part.[26] He begins with a feeling, he says, which develops into something like a sigh. Then he looks around him for the object that is making him sigh; then he "sigh[s] in words." At best, he goes on, he finds a word or several words that become key to the feeling, and he builds on them to complete the statement. "It's simply by a process of association that I find what the rest of the statement is, what can be collected around that word, what that word is connected to." He then demonstrates the process specifically:

> Partly by simple association, the first thing that comes to my mind like "Moloch is" or "Moloch who," and then whatever comes out. But that also goes along with a definite rhythmic impulse, like DA de de DA de de DA de de DA DA. "*Mo*loch whose *eyes* are a *thous*and blind *windows*." And before I wrote "Moloch whose eyes are a thousand blind windows," I had the word, "Moloch, Moloch, Moloch," and I also had the feeling DA de de DA de de DA de de DA DA. So it was just a question of looking up and seeing a lot of windows, and saying, oh, windows, of course, but what kind of windows? But not even that—"Moloch whose eyes." "Moloch whose *eyes*"—which is beautiful in itself—but what about it, Moloch whose eyes are *what*? So Moloch whose eyes—then probably the next thing I thought was "thousands." O.K., and then thousands *what*? "Thousands blind." And I had to finish it somehow. So I hadda say "windows." It looked good *afterward*.

Ginsberg emphasizes the word "*afterward*" because the spontaneity of his poetry depends upon the Existential formula: existence precedes essence. While Ginsberg is writing, he is living (existing) through the experience. Thought *about* that experience (essence) would reduce the immediacy of the experience itself—even make it secondhand—and so, as Ginsberg says, "usually during the composition, step by step, word by word and adjective by adjective, if it's at all spontaneous, I don't know whether it even makes sense sometimes." [27] Spontaneity seems to require suspension of the rational faculties for the purpose of permitting the logic of the heart to operate freely. Testimony for this assertion is Ginsberg's own: "Sometimes I do know it makes complete sense, and I start crying." [28] Clearly, *Howl*, like most of Ginsberg's work, follows a grammar of emotion. The "verification principle" is shifted from the logical positivists' tests:—Can I see it, smell it, taste it, hear it, or feel it?—to the simplest test of the heart: "Does it make me cry?"

Any analysis or explication of *Howl* would seem to be an affront to the poem's own method which is literally a violent howl of spontaneous, supra-rational feeling. Ex post facto explanation almost appears a certain way of completely missing the point. Nevertheless, a few generalizations and observations may prove to be helpful guideposts through this "animal cry" of human anguish. First of all, the poet sets himself up as observer in the opening line. He is witness to the destruction of "the best minds of my generation" by madness (9). "Madness" presumably is the state of civilization which the poet understands as hostile to the sentient martyrs whose collective experiences under the tyranny of that civilization are catalogued in a cumulative, cresting wave of relative clauses. Second, at the same time, madness occurs thematically in the first part of the poem in other forms. For example, it is suggested that these martyrs have been attracted to what is implied as a mad quest: they are "burning for the ancient heavenly connection to the starry dynamo in the machinery of the night," and they have "bared their brains to Heaven" (9). Farther along in the poem it is mentioned that they "thought they were *only* mad when Baltimore gleamed in supernatural ecstasy [italics mine]" (11), which is later followed by a reference to Ginsberg's own commitment to an asylum (15), and finally the specific application of the madness theme to a specific individual, Carl Solomon, who is undergoing treatment at Rockland State Hospital (16).

There is a degree of ambivalence in the use of this crucial term "madness" in the first line. Does it reflect merely the "madness" of an officially acceptable level of reality which is uncongenial to the suffering heroes of the poem, or is it not possible that this destructive "madness" is also a term which describes the predicament of nonconformists? In other words, are not these martyrs self-destroyed because they refuse to live on the acceptable plane of official reality? In these terms, the "angelheaded hipsters" are embracing "madness" as an alternative to an unbearable sanity. Their madness consists in their refusal to accept a non-spiritual view of the world, in their "burning for the ancient heavenly connection" in a civilization that has proclaimed that God is dead. For this reason, Ginsberg emphasizes their thinking "they were *only* mad when Baltimore gleamed in supernatural ecstasy" (11).[29]

At any rate, a tension is created in the poem between planes of reality which are differentiated in terms of time. The "hipsters" undergo a pilgrimage through "blind streets of shuddering cloud and lightening of the mind" (9) which illuminates "all the motionless world of Time, between/Peyote solidities of halls . . ." (10), and so on. This time is supernatural, eternal—not the chronological time of unilluminated existence. Peyote is a chemical channel to timelessness, and the "lightening in the mind" is a "*petite sensation*" which is a gap in time itself. Among other things, the "hipster" pilgrimage is a journey out of time and the insufferable plane of reality it represents. Because of this journey, they "threw their watches off the roof to cast their ballot for Eternity outside of Time, & alarm clocks fell on their heads every day for the next decade" (13). For pursuing "timelessness," the "hipsters" are punished by "Time"; and the symbol of the tyrannical alarm clocks is particularly effective because of their association with the humdrum, inhuman requirements of the "square world."

Christian parallels are unavoidable. The persecution of the early followers of Christ in Roman catacombs finds its counterpart in the despair of those "who lit cigarettes in boxcars boxcars boxcars racketing through snow toward lonesome farms in the grandfather night" (11), and those "who were burned alive in their innocent flannel suits on Madison Avenue amid blasts of leaden verse . . . or were run down by the drunken taxicabs of Absolute Reality" (14). Finally, there is Carl Solomon, the supreme martyr —the archetype who is "really in the total animal soup of time" (16)—to whom the poem is addressed.

Part two of *Howl*, written under the influence of Peyote, is an accusation: "What sphinx of cement and aluminum bashed open their skulls and ate up their brains and imagination?" (17). The protagonist "who" is now replaced, in an attempt to coordinate the structures of the two sections, by the antagonist "Moloch." [30] The spontaneity of this part is vitiated not so much because Ginsberg violates the principles of rapid associations and the like, but because the element of surprise is gone. The unraveling of the *J'accuse* is painfully inevitable, and Ginsburg is thrown back upon the single resource of imagery. The effect of the *petites sensations* has by this time been blunted almost to the point of tedium, and the voice of the propagandist begins to usurp that of the poet. The case is almost identical with the much-criticized Usury canto of Ezra Pound of which Karl Shapiro laments: "Pound sentimentalizing over usury in Quakerish English is almost too painful to read." [31] Without the sauce of the unexpected, Ginsberg's Hebraic lamentations on Moloch become increasingly difficult to digest as they drag on to the inevitable conclusion where the "Mad generation" is hurled "down on the rocks of Time" (18).

Part three begins suspiciously like a "pep talk" or a get-well card: "Carl Solomon! I'm with you in Rockland where you're madder than I am" (19). Whether this assertion is diagnosis or flattery hinges on the connotation one chooses for "madness." Solomon, however, has been raised, through the bulk of accumulation, to the status of a symbol. The final section of the poem unfolds as a dark version of Donne's *Seventeenth Meditation.* Certainly, "no man is an island," but Donne never could have anticipated such lines as "I'm with you in Rockland where we hug and kiss the United States under our bedsheets," or "I'm with you in Rockland where you accuse your doctors of insanity and plot the Hebrew socialist revolution against the fascist national Golgotha . . ." (20).

Whether the following explanation of the total pattern of *Howl* was premeditation or afterthought, even Ginsberg would probably decline to say; but it does supply a workable rationale for the project and deserves acknowledgment: "Part I, a lament for the Lamb in America with instances of remarkable lamblike youths; Part II names the monster of mental consciousness that preys on the Lamb; Part III a litany of affirmation of the Lamb in its glory: 'O starry-spangled shock of Mercy!' The structure of Part III, pyramidal, with a graduated longer response to the fixed base." [32]

Ginsberg considers "Footnote to *Howl*" as the last of a series of experiments with a fixed base. "I set it as Footnote to *Howl* because it was an extra variation of the form of Part II," [33] he explains. "Moloch," the symbol of social illness, was the metrical anchor in Part II for a series of graphic but predictable images. Since "Footnote" presumes to offer a cure for the social illness (Moloch), it is appropriate that the structure of both sections be roughly parallel and that the word "Holy" should operate in the same manner as its counterpart, "Moloch." In this way a symmetrical balance is achieved both structurally and thematically. A simple comparison of a line from each section picked at random immediately shows Ginsberg's conscious exploitation of structural balance for thematic purposes:

> Moloch whose eyes are a thousand blind windows! Moloch whose
> skyscrapers stand in the long streets like endless Jehovahs!

> Moloch whose factories dream and croak in the fog!
> Moloch whose smokestacks and antennae crown the cities! (17)
>
> . . . .
>
> Holy the solitudes of skyscrapers and pavements! Holy the cafeterias filled with millions! Holy the mysterious rivers of tears under the streets! (21)

Clearly, the distinction between "Moloch" and "Holy" is point of view. One is confronted with identical raw material in both cases (skyscrapers, pavements, and urban commonplaces), but the subjective perspective yields two separate appraisals. On the one hand, there is ugliness; on the other, an understanding of the holiness of everything. The response depends upon how one looks at the world.

If Moloch is a state of mind which is the dark side of a holy state of mind, how does one differentiate between the two attitudes with any precision? Ginsberg once again appears to resort to Time as his touchstone. Part II ends in a rhetorical fury which describes, among a plethora of other things, a "Mad generation! down on the rocks of Time!" (18). Similarly, "Footnote" contains near its conclusion the somewhat enigmatic line:"Holy time in eternity holy eternity in time holy the/clocks in space holy the fourth dimension holy the/fifth International holy the Angel in Moloch!"

Obviously, the two distinct understandings of time are exhibited in these lines: on the one hand, there is a destructive time which belongs to the realm of Moloch and which scuttles the "mad generation" upon its craggy surface; on the other hand, there is the paradoxical time of holiness, where time and eternity (logical opposites) are reconciled presumably in the "fourth dimension." To simplify an excessively complicated idea, it appears that Ginsberg is merely attempting to differentiate between an objective, chronological timekeeping, with its attendant implications of responsibility, duty, competition, and the like, and a subjective, Bergsonian temporal measurement which understands time only as it is relative to human existence. Time, therefore, becomes a symbol of two separate realms of existence: the "square" reads time on his wristwatch; the "hipster" reads the holy "clocks in space" which tell him that time does not matter—that the truth is timeless.

The concern for objective time, then, is not merely a symptom of Moloch's activity in the world; it is the very activity itself. Time is the natural enemy of holiness because holiness is discovered through love. One need go no further than traditional love poetry to be convinced that time is the natural opponent of love, but Ginsberg presumes to carry this natural antagonism to its extreme by implying that the modern obsession with objective time prevents one from experiencing a true community with one another. The enigmatic assertion in "Footnote"—"Who digs Los Angeles IS Los Angeles" (21)—serves to sum up, in a way, Ginsberg's whole attitude toward time. Time, to Ginsberg, is always present tense because he acknowledges only time which is "lived through." Los Angeles, for example, is not just a place existing at a certain time; Los Angeles is a human being's concerned impression of Los Angeles. For that concerned person, Los Angeles exists only when he is "digging" it. In that sense, the individual is a solipsist of sorts who creates the reality of Los Angeles in his mind, timeless and placeless, holy and eternal.

III *Other Poems*

Along with the notorious *Howl* in this volume are also several other poems of significance. One of the best, "In the Baggage Room at Greyhound," has already been discussed, but also of some interest are "Sunflower Sutra" and "America." "Sunflower Sutra" (28–30) has been somewhat anticipated by an earlier poem included in the volume and called "In back of the real" (44). The themes of both poems are essentially the same, but "In back of the real" exhibits an early experiment with the short line while its "Sunflower Sutra" demonstrates the later long-line method. Both poems involve flowers seen against backdrops of a railroad yard in San Jose and a "tincan banana dock," respectively. In "In back of the real," the flower is seen as a symbolic martyr ("It had a/brittle black stem and corolla of yellowish dirty/spikes like Jesus' inchlong crown. . . .") That suffers under the oppressive grime of industrialization. It is a "flower of industry, tough spikey ugly flower." Both Jesus and the flower are understood as bearing the sins of man, the adjective "spikey" even suggesting a vague allusion to the stigmata. The point of the poem, which the title explicitly proclaims, is that, despite the ugliness of the exterior of the flower, it is a "flower nonetheless, with the form of the great yellow Rose in your brain!/This is the flower of the World."

The word "real" in the title is meant to represent only the external appearance of an inherent, natural reality of "flowerness" which remains constant underneath the filth of civilization. In *back* of the real (the ugliness) the poet finds an almost platonic formal reality, and the situation of the flower is seen to be an emblem of the present human situation. In short, the theme is hardly different than the theme of "Footnote to *Howl*" where it is proclaimed that "Everything is holy" in its root nature and is discoverable through love.

The similar themes of the earlier and the later poems permit one to appreciate some of the radical effects that are achieved with the introduction of the long line. The later poem, "Sunflower Sutra," is a complete metamorphosis and, for those appreciative of what Ginsberg is trying to achieve, a far more genuine article. Why? The first poem is spare, economical, and contains the striking comparison of the flower with Christ. Although it is written in the first person, the general tone is rather formal. The focus of attention is upon the flower, not upon the perceiver of the flower. In short, the poem has the rudiments of a classical quality to it—classical, at least, within the limitations that William Carlos Williams would set around the term. The short line has obviously produced the presence of a control throughout the fabric of the poem. The control saturates the structure and even permeates to the treatment of what is intended as a highly personal epiphany.

Contrast this feeling of control with "Sunflower Sutra," and the tremendous difference between a relatively good early Ginsberg poem and a relatively good later Ginsberg poem can be seen in an instant. The distinction totally transcends structure, but structure is its genesis. The intimacy of the first person, to begin with, is expanded through the introduction of a second persona—Jack Kerouac. The description of the scene (which is structurally a *sine qua non* in both poems) is developed much more expansively, because of the meditative possibilities of the long line. Dramatic narrative enters the poem, increasing the immediacy and personal intimacy of the moment, so that, when the flower is discovered ("Look at the Sunflower, he said . . . I rushed up enchanted . . ."), a kinetic energy is released that begins a buildup of emotion impossible in the earlier poem. Finally, there is no hint of artifice in "Sunflower Sutra." It is completely natural and completely in the present. There is no scavenging of the past for significant allusions; the immediate ingredients of what is under the nose accomplish everything without assistance, save for the sermon which concludes the poem and makes *ex*plicit what was *im*plicit in "In back of the real."

The transition from the short-line form to the long, with its attendant changes in tone, charts the course of Ginsberg's poetry from what might be termed conventional, literary verse to Kerouac's ideal of "Spontaneous prose." As Ginsberg has said, "Of course the distinctions between prose and poetry are broken down anyway. So much that I was saying like a long page of oceanic Kerouac is sometimes as sublime as epic line." [34] What Ginsberg finds so attractive in the long line is, therefore, its possibilities for honestly and without deception telling the truth about things (which for Ginsberg is, at this stage in his life, inward). The formal devices of traditional poetry, as have been seen, are for him hypocrisy. For these reasons Ginsberg was so astounded, as he reports it, when Kerouac told him one night "that in the future literature would consist of what people actually wrote rather than what they tried to deceive other people into thinking they wrote, when they revised it later on." [35]

"America" (31–34)—about as spontaneous as a poem can be—is whimsical, sad, comic, tedious, honest, bitter, impatient and yet, somehow, incisive. It refuses to settle on a consistent structure. Dialogue discovers that it is monologue and then drifts off into mutterings against a hypothetical national alter ego. The poem is an attempt to catch the mood of a particular attitude toward the United States without the interference of logic. It is a drunken poet arguing after hours with a drunken nation; and yet, through all the turmoil, the gibberish, and the illogicality, a broad-based attack is launched against American values that rational discourse could only hint at. The seemingly hopeless illogicality of the poem itself becomes a mirror for the hopeless illogicality it reflects.

Interspersed throughout the poem are lines that suggest almost all of the attitudes, postures, and convictions that have already been discovered in Ginsberg's other poems. First and foremost is the souring of Whitman's exuberant optimism toward America into a disillusionment that suggests the breaking of a covenant:

"America I've given you all and now I'm nothing" (31). This admission is followed later in the poem by an appeal to America to shake off its hypocrisy and be equal to Whitman's challenge: "America when will you be angelic?/When will you take off your clothes?" (31). The Existential death motif, which sees death as the illumination of the potentialities of life, comes directly afterward ("When will you look at yourself through the grave?"), which is shortly followed by the here-and-now position previously articulated in the poem "Metaphysics": "America after all it is you and I who are perfect not the next world" (31).

The characteristic Zen antagonism toward striving and competition is also represented significantly in "America":

> I'm obsessed by Time Magazine.
> . . . .
> It's always telling me about responsibility. Business men
> are serious
> Movie producers are serious. Everybody's serious
> but me. (32)

And so the poem continues in a jerky dialogue full of shifting issues, which only at the conclusion bothers to justify its nonsensical logic and its logical nonsense: "America this is the impression I get from looking in the television set./America is this correct?" (34)

The real impact of the protest in this poem is conveyed *structurally*. The scattered irritations and objections are merely instrumental caprice; it is the total bewilderment and confusion that one *feels* in reading the poem rather than the validity of the attacks which quickens one's appreciation of the American dilemma which Ginsberg attempts to mirror.

"A Supermarket in California" (23) is another study of the contrasts between Whitman's America and Ginsberg's. True to the American idiom, the poet is pictured as "shopping for images" in the "supermarket" of American life, dreaming all the while of Whitman's "enumerations." Here is poet as consumer filling his shopping cart for the ingredients of his art among "Aisles full of husbands!" Implicit in his meditations is the question: What would Whitman have thought of his America now? A dramatic reconstruction takes place: "I saw you, Walt Whitman, childless, lonely old grubber,/poking among the meats in the refrigerator and eyeing the/grocery boys."

The poet follows Whitman "in and out of the brilliant stacks of cans" (follows him also, in fact, in poetic technique), imaginatively feeling the presence of the "store detective" behind them. Even here, Ginsberg cannot help underscoring the illicitness of the poet's position in society—both his own and Whitman's. No doubt Ginsberg's many brushes with the authorities have helped to nourish his obsession that the way of the true poet inevitably arouses police suspicion. But the poet can always enjoy the freedom of his own mind, which is suggested in the following lines: "We strode down the open corridors together in our/solitary fancy tasting artichokes, possessing every frozen/delicacy, and never passing the cashier" (23). Fortunately, images don't cost anything; they have already been paid for by those who have put them up for display, and this fact leads to the final meditation of the last stanza.

"Where are we going, Walt Whitman? The doors close in an hour. Which way does your beard point tonight?" Ginsberg asks. The urgency of the *Quo vadis?* adds pathos to the appeal. There is not much time. What are the options old "graybeard"? Will they continue their alien course? "Will we walk all night through solitary streets? . . . we'll both be lonely." Or will the poet and Whitman give up on their country and "stroll dreaming of the lost America of love past blue automobiles in driveways, home to our silent cottage"? Despair and nostalgia seem the two alternatives, and the disciple is bewildered.

The poem ends, as it inevitably must, with a question: "Ah, dear father, graybeard, lonely old courage-teacher,/what America did you have when Charon quit poling his ferry/and you got out on a smoking bank and stood watching the/boat disappear on the black waters of Lethe?" (24). Obviously, Whitman's America was quite different from the one Ginsberg sees about him, and the next poem in the collection, "Transcription of Organ Music" (25–27), follows Ginsberg "home to our silent cottage" where he ponders his Existential misery to a Zen beat.

The poem is quite simply the description of a moment—a timeless moment when an event occurs. The event is nothing more sensational than "a moment of clarity" when the poet "saw the feeling in the heart of things [and] walked out into the garden crying." The moment sounds very similar to one of Wordsworth's "time spots" or mystic visions, but the reference in Ginsberg's poem is decidedly Oriental. The mood is what in Zen would be called *wabi*, an instance which, in Alan Watts's words, is "when the artist is feeling depressed or sad, and in this particular emptiness of feeling catches a glimpse of something rather ordinary and unpretentious in its incredible 'suchness.' " [36]

The opening two-line stanza roughly approximates two *haiku* poems and serves as a kind of introduction, or perhaps frame, for the body proper of the work:

> The flower in the glass peanut bottle formerly in the kitchen
> crooked to take a place in the light,
> the closet door opened, because I used it before, it kindly
> stayed open waiting for me, its owner. (25)

Then comes the articulation of the *wabi:* "I began to feel my misery in pallet on floor, listening to music, my misery, that's why I want to sing."

Two things are of paramount importance to understanding the movement of this poem. One is the expectation of "the presence of the Creator" (*satori*), and the other is the attempt to dissolve all conflict between man and nature. The medium in which both of these phenomena occur is timelessness—the absence of hurry, rush, urgency, when "the human senses are fully open to receive the world." [37] The beginning of the "moment of clarity" occurs when the poet, listening to the music, realizes that his "gray painted walls and ceiling" contained him "as the sky contained . . . [his] garden." An equation is grasped between himself and nature which is understood particularly in flowers.

In attempting to transcribe the affinity, even the oneness, between himself and flowers, he runs into the Zen problem of creation; for, according to the principles of Zen, to expend effort in creation is to lose precisely the ability to create. As the poem puts it, "Can I bring back the words? Will thought of transcription haze my mental open eye?" (25) Thinking is not the answer to transcription here, for "the Taoist mentality makes, or forces, nothing but 'grows' everything." [38] Hence, Ginsberg's next line becomes clear: "the kindly search for growth, the gracious desire to exist of/the flowers, my near ecstasy at existing among them. . . ." The problem, then, is not to write about a flower or an experience of a flower, but to become a flower. Zen masters, supervising the art training of their pupils, watch their students as "a gardener watches the growth of a tree, and wants his student to have the attitude of the tree." [39]

Time and the responsibilities that time imply are foreign to this moment, and so books on the table are described as "waiting in space where I placed them, they haven't disappeared, time's left its remains and qualities for me to use" (25). This is a moment, in other words, expanded, but not endless. Time has literally stopped in order that an "openness" to things can occur. As Watts observes, "It is only when there is no goal and no rush that the human senses are fully open to receive the world," [40] and this is precisely what happens during the "glimpse of clarity" in the poem. It is a celebration of "openness" to the world which is structurally held together by the initial and subsequent references to the open closet door. "I looked up," the poet says, "those red bush blossoms . . . their leaves . . . upturned top flat to the sky to receive—all creation open to receive . . ." (26).

There are other "openings" as well—a catalogue of them. There is a light socket open "to receive a plug which . . . serves my phonograph now . . ."; the doorless entry to the kitchen; "the door to the womb was open to admit me if I wished to enter"; the "unused electricity plugs all over my house if I ever need them"; the open kitchen window. Significantly, only the potential openness of the telephone is non-functional at this moment; the telephone is an openness to time which is for the present suspended. This enumeration of "connections" Ginsberg provides for his own consideration—connections that bind together man and nature, nature and the cosmos. It is Ginsberg's way of expressing the Zen insight that "if we open our eyes and see clearly, it becomes obvious that there is no other time than this instant, and that the past and the future are abstractions without any concrete reality." [41] The poet Hung Tzu-ch'eng puts it thus:

> If the mind is not overlaid with wind and waves, you will always be living among blue mountains and green trees. If your true nature has the creative force of Nature itself, wherever you may go, you will see fishes leaping and geese flying.[42]

CHAPTER 5

Kaddish

ALLEN Ginsberg once said that "Everything I write is in one way or another autobiographical or present consciousness at the time of writing." [1] No single opus in the Ginsberg canon demonstrates the truth of this assertion better than *Kaddish*. Intensely autobiographical and intensely present in its projection, *Kaddish* can safely be designated as Ginsberg at his purest and perhaps at his best. The dramatic intimacy of the narrative is poignant; but, more than that, the formal nature of the poem as prayer suggests its relevance to the phenomenon that "man prays to a God whom he does not understand, a fact which to a large extent reflects the nature of the prayer, namely, *telling God that one does not understand.*" [2] One or two lines in *Kaddish* illustrate the anguish which attends such communication with the enigmatic: "Lord Lord great Eye that stares on All and moves in a black cloud . . ." (36) or "Lord Lord and echo in the sky and wind through ragged leaves the roar of memory . . ." (36).

The implicit confession of ignorance toward God precipitates self-understanding, on the part of the one offering the prayer, through the medium of memory—recollection. Hence, this prayer-poem, while it certainly must be considered as calculated reminiscence, becomes at the same time what Ginsberg insists is part of his creative activity: "present consciousness at the time of writing." The function of memory as it operates in this poem is *self*-recollection. "I've seen your grave! O strange Naomi!" Ginsberg says, and immediately adds: "My own—cracked grave!" (27). Or in the last section: "Lord Lord Lord Naomi underneath this grass my halflife and my own as her's . . ." (36). History, in this poem, is resuscitated, taken from the tomb of time and given new life, in the "present consciousness." This situation is precisely the sort that Carl Michalson meant when he wrote, "Self-recollection is achieved by encounter with the self-world, the human world of the past, but encounter of a sort that allows the human world to evoke the present as meaningful."[3]

One has, then, in *Kaddish* a mourner's prayer that oddly contains a distinct pragmatic intention of its own. This mercilessly intimate narrative recollection of the deceased mother becomes the glass through which the poet peers darkly into his own existence. At the same time, because of the inevitable interplay between the confident assurance of the "Mourner's Kaddish" of Reformed Judaism and Ginsberg's reworking of the litany, there is great opportunity for irony of the most relevant sort: the irony of the certainty of the official prayer placed against the anguished uncertainty of Man thrown, in the twentieth century, into a secularized world.

Quite obviously, the focal point of this ironic tension centers around the eschatological question which, as has already been seen, Ginsberg grapples with in such poems as "Metaphysics," "In Death, Cannot Reach What is Most Near," and "This is about Death." In *Kaddish*, for example, there is the appeal at the end of Section I: "Death, stay thy phantoms!" (12). What this line appears to be is a resolution to refuse all traditional consolations—to face death as *finality*, to reject the "phantoms" of promises of eternal life. "Blessed be Death on us All" (32) ends Ginsberg's "Hymmnn," which seems to be a poetic version of Norman Mailer's Existential conviction that "the only life-giving answer is to accept the terms of death."[4] In short, Ginsberg's *Kaddish* is an updating of the older, official model, which cleanses, demythologizes, and stays "the phantoms" of the original. It challenges the relevancy of Judaic eschatological orthodoxy which avers: "To the departed whom we now remember, may peace and bliss be granted in life eternal. May they find grace and mercy before the Lord of heaven and earth. May their souls rejoice in that ineffable good which God has laid up for those who fear Him, and may their memory be a blessing unto those who treasure it."[5]

The measure of Ginsberg's suspicion of these phantoms of hope is taken early in the poem:

> To go where? In that Dark—that—in that God? a radiance?
> A Lord in the Void? Like an eye in the black cloud in a dream? Adonoi at last, with you?
> Beyond my remembrance! Incapable to guess! Not merely the

> yellow skull in the grave, or a box of worm dust, and a stained ribbon—Deathshead with Halo? can you believe it? (10)

Obviously, Ginsberg cannot believe; and much of the power of *Kaddish* is generated by the powerful engines of doubt that roar through memory to the final conclusion that "What came is gone forever every time" (9).

Once the break is made with the "phantoms," the poet is left with the only certain reality he has—himself. This experience *Kaddish* reports, and for this reason Ginsberg has written on the overleaf of the fifth edition: "These poems almost un-conscious to confess the beatific human fact, the language intuitively chosen as in trance & dream, the rhythms rising from breath into the breast and belly, the hymn completed in tears, the movement of the physical poetry demanding and receiving decades of life while chanting Kaddish the names of Death in many mindworlds the self seeking the Key to life found at last in our self."

Interestingly enough, this statement was written in 1963, several years after the composition of the poem; it reflects the change that had come about in Ginsberg's philosophical posture in Asia during the year documented in the poem "The Change." [6] The change that Ginsberg underwent is, ex post facto, exceedingly relevant to *Kaddish,* as well as to his constant convictions about poetic prophecy and the intuitive nature of artistic creation. Describing the state of mind he was in prior to the Asian experience, Ginsberg has said that "The psychic problem that I had found myself in was that for various reasons it had seemed to me at one time or another that the best thing to do was to drop dead. Or not to be afraid of death but go into death. Go into the non-human, go into the cosmic so to speak; that God was death, and if I wanted to attain God I had to die." This certainly is the attitude underlying *Kaddish* ("Nameless, One Faced, Forever beyond me, beginningless, endless, Father in death"). [7]

The change that occurred, however, was a distinct deviation from this position which was perhaps anticipated in the tiny cameo poem in *Empty Mirror:*

> I made love to myself
> in the mirror, kissing my own lips,

saying, "I love myself,
I love you more than anybody." (41)

What happened, as Ginsberg describes it, was that "I suddenly didn't want to be *dominated* by that non-human any more, or even be dominated by the moral obligation to enlarge my consciousness any more. . . . I was suddenly free to love myself again, and therefore love people around me, in the form that they already were. And love myself in my own form as I am." [8]

What one finds, therefore, in Ginsberg's comment appended to the fifth edition of *Kaddish,* is a delayed *exposition de texte,* a gloss which reinterprets a prior intuition in terms of a point of view later discovered. It is verification of Ginsberg's faith in poetic prophecy. "What prophecy actually is," Ginsberg feels, "is not that you actually know that the bomb will fall in 1942. It's that you know and feel something which somebody knows and feels in a hundred years. And maybe articulate it in a hint—concrete way that they can pick up on in a hundred years." [9]

Kaddish was written in one long two-day sitting with amphetamine injections "plus a little bit of morphine, plus some dexedrine later on to keep me going." The purpose of the amphetamine, according to Ginsberg, was to give "a peculiar metaphysical tinge to things . . . Space-outs." [10] Although the poem is numerically innumbered into five parts, the actual structure of the poem includes a "Proem, narrative, hymmnn, lament, litany & fugue." No serious attempt seems to have been made to follow specifically any of the traditional forms of the Kaddish ritual, but the general rhythmic and procedural similarities are unmistakable. At one point in Part II a fragment of "The Mourner's Kaddish" is quoted in Hebrew and inserted in the poem: *"Yisborach, v'yistabach, v'yispoar, v'yisroman, v'yisnaseh,/v'yishador, v'yishalleh, v'yishallol, sh'meh dkudsho, b'rich hu."* ("May God remember the soul of our honored mother who is gone to her repose." [24]).

Repose, in Ginsberg's vocabulary, connotes a merciful salvation from life—relief from "All the accumulations of life that wear us out—clocks, bodies, consciousness, shoes, breasts—begotten sons . . ." (11). As an antonym for life, repose is a scarcely disguised death wish, one that evolves from a weariness, even a disgust, with the "vale of tears" life had become. "We are in a fix!" Ginsberg declares to his dead mother. "And you're out, Death let you out, Death had the Mercy, You're done with your century, done with God, done with the path thru it—Done with yourself at last . . ." (9). Ginsberg has no heavenly vision here; the blessing of Death is relief from pain. The triumph of Life is stoic forbearance: "[There is] Nothing beyond what we have—what you had—that so pitiful/—yet Triumph,/to have been here, and changed, like a tree, broken, or flower—/fed to the ground—but mad, with its petals, colored,/thinking Great Universe, shaken, cut in the head, leaf/stript, his in an egg crate hospital, cloth wrapped, sore/—freaked in the moon brain, Naughtless" (10).

Naomi Ginsberg, the archetype of modern man, has not been tragically cut down suddenly like Emily Dickinson's flower beheaded by "The blond assassin." [11] She is, as Ginsberg notes, "No flower like that flower, which knew itself in the garden, and fought the knife—lost/Cut down by an idiot Snowman's fancy" (10–11). Instead, Naomi's demise was slow and tedious, brought on by the dismal accumulations of life which the remainder of the poem documents in stark, horrifying clarity.

As elegy, *Kaddish* voices its protest not against cruel death, but against insane life—or, more to the point, life that drives one insane by its encouragement of mad idealisms and visions of something more. ("The key is in the window, the key is in the sunlight at the window—I have the key—Get married allen don't take drugs—the key is in the bars, in the sunlight in the window" [31]).

The pathetic, autobiographical narrative of Part II requires no explanation. It is the personal diary of a son's witness to his mother's interment under the accumulations of life that wear all to death. It is "*auto*biographical" narrative because the real history presented is not that of Naomi Ginsberg but the history of her son's finding himself in the revitalization of memory. The case is the exact opposite of Sartre's hero in *Nausea*, who, in writing a biography of Rollebon, says of his subject: "He had need of me in order to be, and I had need of him in order not to sense my being." [12] Ginsberg did not lose himself in his account of Naomi and her madness; in a sense, he exploited his recollections of the anguish to help him understand the nature of his own:

> O glorious muse that bore me from the womb, gave
> suck first mystic life and taught me talk and music, from
> whose pained head I first took Vision—

> Tortured and beaten in the skull—What mad hallucinations of the damned that drive me out of my own skull to seek Eternity till I find Peace for Thee, O Poetry—and for all humankind call on the Origin. (29)

The "mad hallucinations of the damned" that Ginsberg speaks of is not a rhetorical extravagance but an acknowledgment of an actual autobiographical experience—his Blake vision. Much of the material in *Kaddish* is directly related to this crucial phenomenon in Ginsberg's life because the experience opened a new level of consciousness to the poet which permitted him to glimpse the possibility of the radical oneness of the world and existence. Using a phrase from Blake's poem, "The Little Girl Lost," ("Then let Lyca wake"), Ginsberg asks himself: ". . . wake to what? *Wake* meaning wake to . . . [the] existence in the entire universe. . . . In other words a breakthrough from ordinary habitual quotidian consciousness into consciousness that was really seeing all of heaven in a flower." [13]

At another point he has called this "a sudden awakening into a totally deeper real universe than I'd been existing in." [14] The psychological result of this vision was a split consciousness—a double vision of the world, or roughly the equivalent of appreciating a noumenal as well as a phenomenal existence. The origin of Naomi's somewhat cryptic advice to her son: "The key is in the window," undoubtedly finds its origin at the moment Ginsberg heard the voice of Blake and peered out his tenement window in Harlem. "Looking out the window," he has said, "through the window at the sky, suddenly it seemed that I saw into the depths of the universe, by looking simply into the ancient sky. . . . And this was the very ancient place that he was talking about, the sweet golden clime, I suddenly realized that *this* existence was *it!*" [15]

It is only natural that such an experience should exploit religious language for adequate expression; and the totality of the experience of the double vision, or the "crack in the consciousness," helps to clarify Ginsberg's commentary appended to *Kaddish:*

> In the midst of the broken consciousness of mid twentieth century suffering anguish of separation from my own body and its

natural infinity of feeling its own self one with all self, I instinctively seeking to reconstitute that blissful union which I experienced so rarely I took it to be supernatural and gave it holy Name thus made hymn laments of longing and litanies of triumphancy of Self over the mind-illusion mechano-universe of unfeeling Time in which I saw myself my own mother and my very nation trapped desolate our worlds of consciousness homeless and at war except for the original trembling of bliss in breast and belly of everybody that nakedness rejected in suits of fear that familiar defenseless living hurt self which is myself same as all others abandoned scared to own our unchanging desire for each other.

Kaddish documents, therefore, the horror of a whole universe that has lost its integrity, its knowledge of the oneness of all selves. Madness is the metaphor, and not just the madness of Naomi and Allen, but the question of the very authenticity of madness! Is it madness to see the universe on a different level of reality as Ginsberg has done or as Naomi has done? The problem is recorded in a line of *Howl:* "Who thought they were *only* mad when Baltimore gleamed in supernatural ecstasy" (11). "If it were only that easy!" says Ginsberg by way of explanation. "In other words it'd be a lot easier if you just were crazy, instead of—then you could chalk it up, 'well I'm nutty'—but on the other hand what if it's all true and you're *born* into this great cosmic universe in which you're a spirit angel." [16]

There is an equation in *Kaddish* between insight into a deeper consciousness of the universe and an allusion to God or the Creator. Ginsberg "gave it [the deeper consciousness]" a "holy Name." Hence, in the "Hymmnn" of *Kaddish,* the "He" who is praised is a highly ambivalent entity. "He" is not at all an orthodox Deity, but existence—Being—itself. But even this is not a sufficient definition, for it is not abstract ontology that Ginsberg makes reference to here; he refers to a personalized human Being—sentient awareness of Existential solidarity; that, indeed, "No man is an island unto himself"; and that one can see all of heaven in a flower.[17]

Part IV of *Kaddish* ends with the line addressed to Naomi: "with your death full of Flowers" (35), and it is clear that the flower symbol is of paramount significance in Ginsberg's poetry. It appears in poem after poem and seems to have found its priority in Ginsberg's hierarchy of values because of its relation to the Blake vision. For Ginsberg was reading Blake's "The Sick Rose" when "the voice" spoke to him. While confessing that he cannot explain it on a verbal level, Ginsberg remarks, "The sick rose is myself or self, or the living body, sick because the mind, which is the worm 'that flies in the night, in the howling storm' . . . is destroying it, or let us say death, the worm as being death, the natural process of death, some kind of mystical being of its own trying to come in and devour the body, the rose." [18]

The tentative equation between the worm, the mind, and death fits neatly in to the Romantic fabric of Ginsberg's outlook. The mind (reason) is destructive since it leads ultimately to the "mind-illusion mechano-universe of un-feeling Time." [19] The worm as death—the natural process of death—reflects the awesome inevitability of change which Ginsberg describes as the "beauty of doom" (76).[20]

How can doom be beautiful? How can Ginsberg finish "Hymmnn" with: "Blessed be Death on us all" (32)? The answer lies in Ginsberg's curious esthetic. "If you get interested in Beauty," he has said,

> then you've latched onto something mysterious inside your soul that grows and grows like a secret insane thought, and takes over completely when you die, and you're IT. . . . Now it's weird enough to be in this human form so temporarily, without huge gangs of people, whole societies trying to pretend that their temporary bread & breasts are the be-all and end-all of the soul's fate, and enforcing this ridiculous opinion with big rules of thought & conduct, bureaucracies to control the soul, FBI's, televisions, wars, politics, boring religions . . . a false America's been getting in the way of realization of Beauty . . .[21]

Death, as a release from the "mechano-universe of un-feeling Time," is an inevitable yielding to that "something mysterious inside your soul"—a "secret insane thought." This view is revised in the later Ginsberg, but it is relevant to *Kaddish*, particularly in the lines:

> Blessed be Thee Naomi in Death! Blessed be Death! Blessed be
> Death!

Blessed be He Who leads all sorrow to Heaven! Blessed be He in the end!
Blessed be He who builds Heaven in Darkness! (32)

The higher level of consciousness which sees the cosmos in timelessness provides a perspective that extracts fear from the mystery of death: ". . . all Earth one everlasting Light in the familiar blackout—no tears for this vision," says Ginsberg toward the end of Part III. "But that the key should be left behind—at the window—the key in the sunlight—to the living—that can take /that slice of light in hand—and turn the door—and look back see/Creation glistening backwards to the same grave, size of universe, size of the tick of the hospital's clock on the archway over the white door . . ." (33).

"Madness," as metaphor, controls the whole of Part IV. The terrifying bifurcation of Naomi's existence—slices in the middle by double vision, seeing the world and seeing the universe simultaneously, and being pulled apart by the tension into insanity—is rendered through the ambivalence of the anchor phrase. "with your eyes." This catalogue is not merely one of horrors, even though the biological attrition to death in the final lines underscores graphically not so much the "*accumulations* of life, that wear us out," but the pitiful *reductio ad nihilo* of a human being. The potentiality of the word "eyes" as homonym serves to universalize a particular terrifying biography. It is not only Naomi's "eyes running naked out of the apartment screaming into the hall," but the "*I's*" of all of us. One might even find, perhaps, in these lines the "Ayes" of one's consent.

I *Beyond Mind Consciousness*

The final page of *Kaddish and Other Poems* contains the following note: "Magic Psalm, The Reply, & The End *record visions experienced after drinking Ayahuasca, an Amazon spiritual potion. The message is: Widen the area of consciousness*" (100). While only these three poems are cited as examples of trance notations, many of the other poems in the volume deal with the relevancy of the counsel: "*Widen the area of consciousness.*" The possibility of multiple levels of consciousness and planes of reality beyond normal rational limits became real to Ginsberg when

Blake spoke to him in Harlem, but such possibilities have, of course, been known to men since prehistory. Erich Fromm, for example, has described man as "tormented by a craving for 'absoluteness,' for another kind of harmony which can lift the curse by which he was separated from nature, from his fellow men, and from himself," [22] and from the theological quarter comes Paul Tillich's observation that "man is finite . . . but man is also aware of his potential infinity. . . ." [23] Ginsberg's own comment on the phenomenon is partially articulated in "Laughing Gas" where he notes:

> It's the instant of going
> into or coming out of
> existence that is
> important—to catch on
> to the secret of the magic
> box
>
> Stepping outside the universe
> by means of Nitrous Oxide
> anesthetizing mind-consciousness. . . . (66–67)

What is at stake here cannot be completely exhausted by the term "mysticism," but it certainly partakes of mysticism's intention to probe beyond what Ginsberg calls "mind-consciousness." Traditional mystics—the purists—must deplore Ginsberg's biochemical assaults upon the ineffable; and "Laughing Gas" certainly documents the perils of narcotic undiscipline in such ventures. Real mystics might shake their heads knowingly at Ginsberg's frustration in finding the mind "an irrational traffic light in Gobi" (69), but they would certainly assent to his proposition that

> The universe is a void
> in which there is a dreamhole
> The dream disappears
> the hole closes (66)

Mystic experience is transient, for the hole is always closing. The glimpse is all that can be hoped for; but, once the glimpse has been seen, the soul seeks the repeat performance. So unbearable is the desire for Ginsberg that his life becomes committed to a constant quest through whatever avenues he finds at hand. For a significant portion of his career, drugs have served the purpose. In answer to the question if his use of drugs was an extension of his Blake experience, Ginsberg replied: ". . . drugs were obviously a technique for experimenting with consciousness, to get different areas and different levels and different similarities and different reverberations of the same vision. . . . There are certain moments under laughing gas and æther that the consciousness does intersect with something similar—for me—to my Blake visions."[24]

There is a connection, therefore, among a majority of the poems in the *Kaddish* volume which can roughly be described as attempts to induce mystic flights. The place to begin an examination of this connection is the poem "The Lion for Real" (53–55), which is an allegorical presentation of Ginsberg's original Blake vision. The poem version of the experience itself adds little that has not been dealt with in Ginsberg's prose accounts except that the objectification of the "voice" into animal form has the effect of focusing the emotional power of the vision into an awesome, even savage, intensity. "Terrible Presence!" the poet cries, "Eat me or die!" (55). A frightening dimension of newly perceived reality is confronted. Theologically, the experience would fall under the Judeo-Christian concept of the "wrath of God"; Ginsberg's reaction to it reflects a similar sense of cosmic threat: "[The lion] said in a gravelly voice 'Not this time Baby—but I will be back again' " (55).

One cannot escape the religious depth of the event as it is depicted in verse. Donne's famous Holy sonnet comes immediately to mind:

> Batter my heart, three person'd God; for, you
> As yet but knocke, breathe, shine and seeke to mend,
> that I may rise, and stand, o'erthrow mee, and bend
> Your force, to breake, blowe, burn and make me new.
>
> . . .
>
> for I
> Except you enthrall mee, never shall be free,
> nor ever chast, except you ravish mee.[25]

Ginsberg's poem contains no petition to the "Terrible Presence!" other than the appeal to do his worst ("Eat me or die!") and get it over with; but the power of the Presence is acknowledged as a God, and that power is irresistible:

> Lion that eats my mind now for a decade knowing only
> your hunger
> Not the bliss of your satisfaction O roar of the Universe
> how am I chosen
> In this life I have heard your promise I am ready to die
> I have served
> Your starved and ancient Presence O Lord I wait in my
> room at your Mercy. (55)

The Presence is a salutary demon. Like the "Cruel Fair" of Petrarchan sonneteering, it attracts but never offers satisfaction. The victimized devotee starvingly awaits the dubious promise of mercy.

The anguish of worshiping such a Presence is provoked by the fact of its transiency. It is a mystic glimpse—"Just a flash in the cosmic pan"—and there is no certitude of its authenticity. "The whole universe a shaggy dog story! with a weird ending that begins again till you get the point . . ." (69). Worse, there may be no point at all:

> An endless cycle of possibilities clashing in Nothing
> with each mistake in the writing inevitable from the
> beginning of time
> The doctor's phone number is Pilgrim 1–0000
> Are you calling me, Nothing? (76)

Ginsberg, as pilgrim, is faced with the dizzy possibilities of Nothingness—a classic Existential situation which calls for something akin to the Kierkegaardian "leap of faith." Hence, one has his "decade knowing only your [the lion's] hunger" (55).

Thus, "The Lion for Real" inevitably leads in *Kaddish* to "Laughing Gas" (66–82), and "Laughing Gas" to "Mescaline" (83–85), "Lysergic Acid" (86–91), "Magic Psalm" (92–95), "The Reply" (96–98), and "The End" (99). A wild and often unpleasant pilgrimage, but pilgrimage it is, even literally so; for it takes Ginsberg to the outlands of Peru in search of *Yage,* the drug to end all drugs. "Thank you, O Lord, beyond my eye," says Ginsberg in "Mescaline," "the path must lead somewhere . . ." (83).

II *Poem as Prayer*

"Magic Psalm" is particularly intriguing because of its kinship with a genre of literature which might be called "poetry of religious anguish" that is of a kind with the poems of spiritual torment written by such Christian writers as John Donne, George Herbert, and Gerard Manley Hopkins. The relationship to the Holy Sonnet of Donne alluded to previously is strikingly evident in this passage from Ginsberg:

> Drive me crazy, God I'm ready for disintegration of my mind . . .
> attack my hairy heart with terror . . .
> devour my brain . . .
> Descend O Light Creator & Eater of Mankind . . . (93)

Perhaps even more informative is the device of the naming of "God" which Ginsberg uses as his metrical anchor. The poem begins with a long catalogue of evocations that is so comprehensive that soon a cumulative suggestion of what Ginsberg means by the "Terrible Presence" begins to emerge. He is called:

> O Phantom that my mind pursues from year to year . . .
> Giant outside Time . . .
> Unspeakable Kind of the roads that are gone . . .
> Unintelligible Horse riding out of the graveyard . . .
> Griever . . . Laugh with no mouth, Heart that never had flesh to die—Promise that was not made . . .
> Reliever . . . Destroyer of the World . . . Creator of Breasted Illusions . . . (92)

To this Being, a petition is made in various forms to disrupt rationality ("devour my brain . . ."), as well as the corporate rationality of civilization which is identified as evil ("disrupt the world in its madness of bombs and murder . . ." [93]).

As prayer, the poem directs its appeals most significantly to "Beauty invisible to my century" (94) and asks this deity for the power to evoke a prayer that passes even the author's understanding. This prayer then unfolds, toward the end of the poem, into a series of specific requests that probe to the very core of Ginsberg's concern:

that I surpass desire for transcendency and enter the calm
water of the universe
that I ride out this wave, not drown forever in the flood of
my imagination
that I not be slain thru my own insane magic . . . (94)

This triad of petitions outlines Ginsberg's dilemma. The first suggests his need for peace, for the decade of pilgrimage initiated by the Blake vision has worn him down. The mad quest for the transcendent, which was also the fate of Naomi, is seen as a destructive force within him that must be overcome. Peace must be made with the universe and with existence; and, quite possibly, the serenity of the Tao is the true object of the appeal.

The second appeal is a call for help from a man drowning in his own imagination. His thoughts are torments that lead him he knows not where. The third request follows accordingly that death be not the outcome of his "insane magic" (94). Precisely what this "insane magic" is, is Ginsberg's alleged God-given mission to prophesy, which becomes evident in a final appended appeal that "men understand my speech out of their own Turkish heart,/the prophets aid me with Proclamation,/the Seraphim acclaim Thy Name, Thyself at once in one huge/Mouth of Universe make meat reply" (95).

Under the influence of *Ayahuasca* the messianic energy latent in Ginsberg is given full vent, and the appeal is dramatically underscored by the imperative demand for an answer: ". . . make meat reply." The pun is a happy fruit of invention that combines the urgency of the poet's need for a *proper* answer to his prayer with a suggestion as to the appropriate idiom: through "meat"—the flesh, the humanity, the "sensate transcendency" (92) of the divine essence. This term also corresponds with the earlier request that the Phantom "invade my body with the sex of God" (92).

"The Reply," the companion piece to "Magic Psalm," can be properly appreciated only after digesting the factual account of Ginsberg's experimentation with *Ayahuasca* which he gives in all its terrifying detail in a letter to William Burroughs. The effect of this drug was, in Ginsberg's own words, "the strongest and worst I've ever had it nearly—(I still reserve the Harlem experiences, being natural, in abeyance."[26] The fear that saturates the letter (so great that Ginsberg feels compelled to assure Burroughs at the close of the letter that "everything is OK, I suppose, in case this all just worries you unnecessarily, I'll be all right") is the fear of a man confronting Death. "I felt faced by Death," he wrote to Burroughs, an emotion that becomes poetically transcribed into the opening line of the poem as "God answers with my doom!" (96).

As in most experiences of fear, the triggering ingredient is the unknown:

> I am a Seraph and I know not whither I go into the Void
> I am a man and I know not whither I go into Death——
> Christ Christ poor hopeless
> lifted on the Cross between Dimension—
> to see the Ever-Unknowable! (96)

As far as Ginsberg's basic eschatological problem is concerned—which has already been examined in earlier poems—there is little tangible advance toward a solution. Bede's ancient metaphor of the swallow in flight through the brief light of the illuminated hall still encompasses the boundaries of the dilemma. The emotional volume of the poet's response to the dilemma has been intensified drastically in this poem by the "mind-expanding" properties of the drug. Even the problem of illusion versus reality is deliberately swept aside by Ginsberg in order to meet the experience head-on. "I was frightened," he explained to Burroughs, "and simply lay there with wave after wave of death-fear, fright, rolling over me till I could hardly stand it, didn't want to take refuge in rejecting it as illusion, for it was too real and too familiar. . . ."[27]

As seraph or as man, the fear of "the Void" seems inescapable. The poem appears to document the frenzy of a man who has lifted his head above the waves of temporality expecting to find a "peace which passeth all understanding," but who finds instead the more terrifying cipher of annihilation. "I am annulled" (96), he discovers in "The Reply"; and almost immediately he identifies his experience with Christ who has almost shared his hopeless feeling of being "lifted on the Cross between Dimension" (96).

So much, then, for divine transcendence; for "What's sacred when the Thing is all the universe?" (97). The horrible predicament lies in the fact that there is indeed no exit: "No refuge in Myself, which is on fire/or in the World which is His also to bomb & Devour!" (97). The "faceless Destroyer," which the vision of

God has revealed, is malignantly omnipotent; and the poem ends on the most pessimistic of notes: "The universe turns inside out to devour me!/and the mighty burst of music comes from out the inhuman door—" (98).

Faced with such a dead end, it is inevitable that consolation must come from within; and the concluding poem of the volume, appropriately entitled "The End," seems to herald this message, if in muted tones. The counterreply to "the Thing" is the simple declaration: "I am I, old Father Fisheye that begat the ocean, the worm at my own ear . . ." (99). From this premise follows the humanistic bravado of one uneasily balancing a cosmic chip on his shoulder: "I receive all, I'll die of cancer, I enter the coffin forever,/I close my eye, I disappear . . ." (99). This shaky assertion is bolstered by the familiar standby—Love:

> Love that bore me I bear back to my Origin with no loss,
> I float over the vomiter
> thrilled with my deathlessness, thrilled with this endlessness . . .
> (99)

Curiously, however, the "thrill" of "deathlessness" has no observable source in the poem. The optimistic tag rings hollow, despite an apparently postscriptive appeal to esthetics as the key to the eschatological problem: "come Poet shut up eat my word, and taste my mouth in your ear" (99). The resolution to this problem is not to be bought so cheaply; it requires a trip to Asia, talks with holy men from India, and a conversation with Martin Buber. On this trip Ginsberg learns that the true focus of the difficulty lies in the area of "human relationships rather than relations between the human and the non-human." [28] Hence, in 1963, Ginsberg adds the comment on the flyleaf of *Kaddish and Other Poems:* ". . . the Key to life found at last in our self."

Whatever keys men have found to unlock the doors to existence have traditionally been sought and found in the idea of God as an entity. Clearly, Ginsberg's courtship with drugs has served to objectify an inherent religious need into various magnified entities that reveal themselves as "Terrible Presences" or "Devourers." By taking the option of choosing self over a God-entity, Ginsberg has accomplished what might be called a transition from a transcendent view of deity toward an ontological one. In other words, God-as-entity has proved to be a psychological cul-de-sac; or, as Ginsberg puts it more specifically, "The Asian experience kind of got me out of the corner I painted myself in with drugs." [29] Drugs had taken him as far as he could go in his quest for an objectified God; they had brought him to terror and despair. The final lines of "The End"—"come Poet shut up eat my word, and taste my mouth in your ear"—suggest a new start. The God-entity—the "Terrible Presence"—is supplanted by a more negotiable conception of God as Being. The "I am I" of the first line seems a commitment to existence in its inchoate stage, and this commitment permits Ginsberg to maintain at least one of his feet in the practical world of the here-and-the-now.

III *Van Gogh and Aunt Rose*

An earlier poem, "Death to Van Gogh's Ear!" (61–65) shows how effective Ginsberg can be with clipped wings. The theme is familiar: the usual list of atrocities committed against humanity in the name of "The American Way of Life." The title itself serves as the overlying metaphor: Van Gogh's ear, sliced off by the painter to please a prostitute, is a symbol of irrational, unorthodox behavior, which at the same time is an ultimate human gesture of love. There is a conspiracy against such insane acts which betray the hidden, yet essential, humanity of all men, Ginsberg feels. Hence, the whimsical appeal that America put "Van Gogh's Ear on the currency" (64). The implication is, of course, that the ear is a more viable guide to America's self-realization than "In God We Trust." The creative artist (Van Gogh) is placed in competition with God as the guide to a fitting destiny, and so the poem opens with the assertion: "Poet is Priest."

If the poet *is* priest, his function is to listen to the confessions of the nation. All the confessions which follow in catalogue point to one spiritual disease which is prediagnosed in the second line: "Money has reckoned the soul of America." The rest of the poem is a frenzied complaint centering on the agonizing disparity between the ideal and the real, the human and the inhuman, the spiritual and the material. "The American Century" has been "betrayed by a mad Senate which no longer sleeps with its wife" (61). Government and institutions in general have outgrown love. America is impotent; it is "lacklove."

Industry also comes under priestly wrath: "Detroit has built a million automobiles of rubber trees and phantoms/but I walk, I walk, and the Orient walks with me, and all Africa walks" (61). Trees become machines, and men become parts of machines who no longer walk. Only the Priest himself and the Orient (the mind of Tao?) remain bipeds. The tremendous fertility of America is reduced to barrenness— ". . . mountains of eggs were reduced to white powder in the halls of Congress . . ."—while the rest of the world goes hungry: "aborigines of Australia perhaps gibber in the eggless wilderness/and I rarely have an egg for breakfast tho my work requires infinite eggs to come to birth in Eternity/eggs should be eaten or given to their mothers. . . ."

The poem rises in a crescendo of anger which finally culminates in an outburst which echoes off the shaky walls of the Moloch section of *Howl:*

> Money! Money! Money! shrieking mad celestial money of
> illusion! Money made of nothing, starvation, suicide!
> Money of failure Money of death!
> Money against Eternity! and eternity's strong mills grind out
> vast paper of Illusion! (65)

Nothing more needs be said except for the usual reminder from Ginsberg that he is the voice of the prophet: "History will make this poem prophetic and its awful silliness a/hideous spiritual music . . ." (63).

When the poems in *Kaddish and Other Poems* are not "hideous spiritual music," they often draw on a source of poignant power that proves consistently more reliable than mystic vision. Because they are less pretentious and seemingly less ambitious, they often, as if by accident, hit a chord of such personal intimacy that they become subjects to the single muse of pure poetry. "To Aunt Rose" (46) is one such poem. It is Ginsberg's "Portrait of a Woman" made rich, as *Kaddish* is made rich, by self-discovering memory. It requires no explanation because it is the simple rendering of a woman. An entire existence is somehow evoked with an amazing economy of remembered glimpses and reconstructed insights, and each one of these glimpses is in itself almost capable of capturing the essence of Aunt Rose:

> . . . your tears of sexual frustration
> (what smothered sobs and bony hips
> under the pillows of Osborne Terrace)

Perhaps what separates "To Aunt Rose" from the poems of trance notation is the simple element of control. In the former, admiration is inspired by the confidence that there is a maker behind the poem—that a keen, perceptive discrimination has presented the precise details necessary for capturing a delicate subtlety. The trance-notations do not do this. It is not maker but transcriber that overwhelms the reader with the sound and fury of infinitude in these poems. Relative to this observation is the conviction of Karl Shapiro that "the poet's rapport with God is relatively crude and is like that of the magician and the psychologist rather than that of the mystic. For the poet, the unitive experience is forever blocked by the nature of creative work, art being an embodiment of personality and not a surrender of personality to the larger Being." [30]

CHAPTER 6

Reality Sandwiches and Later Poems

I *The Menu*

GINSBERG'S poem "On Burroughs' Work" concludes with the stanza:

> A naked lunch is natural to us,
> we eat reality sandwiches.
> But allegories are so much lettuce.
> Don't hide the madness. (*Reality Sandwiches* 40)

The title of this fourth volume of collected poems thus pays homage to two of his most influential friends: Jack Kerouac, who suggested "Naked Lunch" as an appropriate title for Burroughs' novel, and, of course, Burroughs himself. Burroughs contends that "[*Naked Lunch*] means exactly what the words say: NAKED Lunch —a frozen moment when everyone sees what is on the end of every fork." [1] *Reality Sandwiches* presumes to exhibit twenty-nine such "frozen moments" that span a full seven years of Ginsberg's development (1953–60).

Both Ginsberg's and Burroughs' titles promise the reader a taste of pure reality and demand that he savor its sweetness and bitterness with a vital palate. Both writers presume to serve an Existential feast devoid of hypocritical condiments which might disguise "the madness." In either case, the program is ambitious and suggests the radical, synesthetic entreaty that Ginsberg once made to Peter Orlovsky when he dedicated *Kaddish and Other Poems* to him: "Taste my mouth in your ear."

The reader gets a good taste of Ginsberg's mouth in his ear in this collection, which, as usual, is uninhibitedly and often flamboyantly honest. As a poetic method, unadulterated honesty is hardly a new departure for Ginsberg. The limits to which honesty have led him are marked by jail sentences, obscenity trials, and a "second-rate creep image that was interpreted to the public via mass media." [2] Honesty has also led him to the lonely regions of isolation where death and self struggle to negotiate a viable program of being. There is much discussion in these poems of what Heidegger would have called the "authentic" versus the "inauthentic" life as well as some further jousting with the problem of Death. The menu is varied and the service is erratic; but, true to his word, Ginsberg is sparing with the lettuce in his sandwiches and the taste of madness is strong.

II *Illuminations*

The initial poem, "My Alba" (7), is an experiment within traditional forms which bears, as do so many of Ginsberg's early verses, a strong affinity to the style of William Carlos Williams. The subject is wasted time, and the method is the catalogue. Williams' poem, "*Le Médecin malgré Lui,*" might easily stand as the model; but Ginsberg thrusts beyond the structural ennui of "*Le Médecin*" to arrive at a description of a human being poised for a spring into authentic existence. It is a morning song that anticipates an awakening. The poet seems to be undergoing the shock of discovering that his life has been non-being; his metaphor is the paraphernalia of the business office. His life is not measured in coffee spoons, but worse: "Sliderule and number/machine on a desk/autographed triplicate/synopsis and taxes. . . ." This catalogue documents a wasted "five years in Manhattan/life decaying/talent a blank."

One successful technique is the sense of boredom that has been created by the incessant run-on lines and by the complete avoidance of punctuation of any kind. The result of the lack of punctuation is an abundance of suggestive liaisons which occur between thought patterns: ". . . Manhattan/life decaying . . . blank/ talking disconnected/patient . . . mental/sliderule. . . ." The feeling that Ginsberg creates and sustains by the use and the structure of language in the body of the poem is decisive in making possible the structural tension that the title lends to the entire poem. The juxtaposition of the awakening, implicit in the title "My Alba," with the ostentatiously banal poem which follows is an example of Ginsberg's borrowing of Williams' typical method of creating significance from structure.

As reinforcement to the structural significance of the poem, Ginsberg also adds a final note of Existential urgency: "I am damned to Hell what/alarmclock is ringing." By this time, the reader realizes that the preceding stanzas have attempted to chart the precincts of Hell and that the ringing of the alarm clock is the sudden awareness of a crisis. The "autographed triplicate/synopsis" is a carbon-copy existence; it is inauthentic, and it is time to awaken to a naked breakfast.

The penultimate stage of illumination that this poem suggests reminds the reader of traditional experiences of religious regeneration in which one is "reborn" to a new understanding of existence. The second selection in this volume, a Zen poem called "Sakyamuni Coming Out from the Mountain," deals with the difficulty of being twice-born: "how painful to be born again/wearing a fine beard,/reentering the world" (10).

The form of this poem seems to be once again derivative from the experiments of William Carlos Williams with the three-step, variable foot line in *Paterson, The Desert Music and Other Poems*, and *Journey to Love*. A single specimen from *Paterson II* suffices to illustrate the similarity:

The descent beckons
        as the ascent beckoned
                Memory is a kind
of accomplishment
        a sort of renewal
                even
an initiation . . .[3]

The obvious characteristics of this style are that each of the three steps is intended to be equal and that, after each step down, there is a caesural pause. The effect is rather like syncopation; the lines come, as John Ciardi has suggested, just "off the beat" of iambic pentameter, and they follow the general rhythmic patterns of modern jazz.[4] For Williams, the method was "a way of escaping the formlessness of free verse,"[5] and the intention was also presumably Ginsberg's. At the same time, however, the Oriental flavor of the poem was an additional concern for Ginsberg, and one could easily make a case for the form's congeniality with *haiku.*

Liang-k'ai was a painter of the Sung dynasty (959–1279), and his work represents a relationship between man and nature which ignores priorities. In other words, his landscapes depict "a world to which man belongs but which he does not dominate." [6] This attitude does much to explain the final declaration of Ginsberg's poem: "humility is beatness/before the absolute World," which in turn provides a nexus to Heidegger's thesis that the predicament of man is that he has been "thrown" into a world with which he must come to terms. Hence, the poem is rich in philosophical possibilities which emerge from a matrix of Taoism, Zen, Beatness, and Existentialism.

The theme of the aimless life, so characteristic of Zen thought, is presented in the opening description of Arhat who "drags his bare feet/out of a cave . . . wearing a fine beard,/unhappy hands/clasped to his naked breast . . . faltering/into the bushes by a stream" (9). The issue of priority between man and nature is then introduced: "all things inanimate/but his intelligence." The function of the intelligence within the context of the Zen attitude is not to separate man from nature but to perform as a receptor of momentary glimpses—glimpses, perhaps, into authentic Being which testify to man's oneness with the world. Humility (Beatness) begins to emerge in the reader's mind as a state whereby a man realizes that he is nothing special in the face of "the absolute World." This recognition seems to be the denouement that the narrative poem offers.

Arhat has been seeking Heaven "under a mountain of stone," and in typical Zen fashion he has "sat thinking" (not imposing his thoughts upon nature, but passively awaiting an understanding) until an awakening occurs. He realizes that "the land of blessedness exists/in the imagination." This realization is analogous to the ringing of an alarm clock, and Arhat is reborn; his "inauthentic" existence is authenticized and he is made humble:

> he knows nothing
> like a god:
> shaken
> meek wretch—(10)

In essence, Ginsberg's poem supplies an answer to one of the fundamental questions that Existentialism poses:

> . . . are we disclosed to ourselves as existents who are always already in a world—a world with which we are concerned and involved in all kinds of ways—so that it is out of this total situation that we must seek after whatever understanding of Being may be possible for us; or are we, as the traditional Western philosophy has been inclined to regard us, primarily thinking subjects, before whom there is spread out for our inspection a world, and this world is to be understood in a genuine way only along the lines of detached theoretical inquiry? [7]

Clearly, "beatness" or "humility" understands only the first option.

"Over Kansas" (42) is another poem which describes a similar illumination, but a contemporary American backdrop replaces the misty forests and lonely rocks of the Sung landscape painters. The situation of the poem is an airplane journey across the United States, one that becomes, in the poet's consciousness, a subjective journey that takes him from ego-less non-being, through a vision of Kansas at night, to a form of self-realization. Two implicit themes seem to embrace in the consummation of this poem: death and nakedness. Death haunts the stanzas in the several references to "death insurance by machine" and the hypothetical poet below in Kansas who is "Someone who should collect/my insurance!" More profoundly, however, death enters the meditations of the traveler as he ponders the fact that he is "Travelling thru the dark void/over Kansas yet moving nowhere/in the dark void of the soul." Death is also present in his mind when he muses that "Not even the human/imagination satisfied/the endless emptiness of the soul."

Clearly, this latter appreciation of death is more than biological: it is a death bred of a man's forgetfulness of what it means to be. Hence, the poem takes an Existential turn which recognizes that anxiety over death brings a new seriousness to life which awakens one to an authentic life. The poet moves from the airport waiting room crowded with businessmen to the dark, isolated sky above "imaginary plains/I never made afoot." He finds himself in "the dark void" above the ground where men actually live, breathe, make love, and "collect the streets and mountain tops/for storage in . . . [their] memory." The illumination comes "in a sudden glimpse" by the poet of his own non-being in the airplane ("me being no one in the air/nothing but clouds in the moonlight . . ."), while underneath him living creatures copulate.

The solution to the dilemma of being versus non-being is summed up in Ginsberg's ubiquitous metaphor: nakedness. All of his poetry is about nakedness, he is always ready to assert; but precisely what "nakedness" means is rarely explained. In this poem, for example, he says, "Nakedness must come again—not sex,/but some naked isolation." This statement seems to suggest an unqualified openness to being, but the sexual suggestiveness of the term is certainly overt in such expressions as "that football boy/in sunny yellow lovesuit. . . ." The reader is also told that "the starry world below [Hollywood]" also expresses nakedness:

> that craving, that glory
> that applause—leisure, mind,
> appetite for dreams, bodies,
> travels: appetite for the real,
> created by the mind
> and kissed in coitus—
> that craving, that melting!

But this is merely an expression of nakedness, imaginary because it is "created by the mind." It is only an appetite for nakedness rather than the real thing, and the reader is immediately informed that "Not even the imagination satisfies/the endless emptiness of the soul."

Then comes the official illumination over Hutchinson, Kansas, where the poet peers beyond his own reflection in the window ("bald businessman with hornrims") and sees a "spectral skeleton of electricity"

> illuminated nervous system
> floating on the void out
> of central brainplant powerhouse
> running into heavens' starlight
> overhead.

The vision is an emblem, presumably. The lights of Hutchinson emanating out of a "central brainplant powerhouse" (the human mind) "floating on the void." Because this "illuminated nervous system" is seen by the poet to be "running into heaven's starlight/ overhead," it seems apparent that "the vision" reveals the potentiality of the human imagination to connect the heavens and this world—in a word, mysticism.

What the reader is up against, then, is the familiar credo of the Angel "hipster." "It'd be a lot easier if you just were crazy," Ginsberg has said, ". . . but on the other hand what if it's all true and you're *born* into this great cosmic universe in which you're a spirit angel. . . .?"[8] After the illumination, the poet is in Chicago between flights and decides that this city is "another project for the heart,"

> six months for here someday
> to make Chicago natural,
> pick up a few strange images.

This spirit angel is on the lookout for missionary work, and it begins to come clear that "nakedness" is merely the unaccommodated man finding in his misery that all are brothers under the skin, that all are angels. In Ginsberg's world, unauthenticated angels rarely fly; their feet trod the dusty earth where life takes place:

> Better I make
> a thornful pilgrimage on theory
> feet to suffer the total
> isolation of the bum,
> than this hipster
> business family journey
> —crossing U.S. at night—

There are so many complex constituents to Ginsberg's illuminations that it is often difficult to analyze or even comprehend precisely the response that is expected. The fact that Ginsberg himself often confesses that he is usually not aware of exactly what he means at the time of writing lends little comfort.[9] Nevertheless, even when exegesis fails, communication of a sort often breaks through. Graffiti collectors are reported to have uncovered this interesting specimen in a men's lavatory: "Ginsberg revises!" If the legend were true, perhaps the task of the explicator would be simplified. For good or for bad, Ginsberg does not write for expositors but for angels; and one must be alert to Wordsworth's counsel that "We murder to dissect."

"Sather Gate Illumination" (54–58) may not present as many problems as "Over Kansas," but the honest lyricism of its celebration of a moment in space and in time manages to avoid the straining for effect that many of the poems in *Reality Sandwiches* exhibit. The poem is Whitman-inspired through and through from the gracious "Dear Walter, thanks-for-the-message" tribute in the beginning to the illumination proper at the end: "Seeing in people the visible evidence of inner self thought by their treatment of me: who loves himself loves me who love myself." Almost any line picked at random from "Song of Myself" serves to explicate the general theme of Ginsberg's piece:

> I CELEBRATE myself, and sing myself,
> And what I assume you shall assume,
> For every atom belonging to me as good belongs to you.

or

> There was never any more inception than there is now,
> Nor any more youth or age than there is now,
> And will never be any more perfection than there is now,
> Nor any more heaven or hell than there is now.

Even more informative are the lines: "Clear and sweet is my soul, and clear and sweet is all that is not my soul/Lack one lacks both, and the unseen is proved by the seen,/Till that becomes unseen and receives proof in its turn." [10]

"Dear Walter's" message is no stopgap communiqué for Ginsberg, but a program of positive perception as well as a healthy dose of self-vindication. It reaffirms the brotherhood of angels: "Why do I deny manna to another?/Because I deny it to myself" (54). The key to the illumination is the acceptance of self which the poem affirms from the start: "Now I believe you are lovely, my soul, soul of Allen, Allen—/and you so beloved, so sweetened, so recalled to your true loveliness,/your original nude breathing Allen/will you ever deny another again?"

There is precious little that is new so far as content is concerned in this poem, and its effect probably rests on the fact that the poet's mind has been liberated for mere observation. There is a dazzling array of commonplace scenes and incidents raised to significance by the slender support of Whitman's insight and buttressed by poetic sensitivity. There is also moral tension structurally built into the poem by the leitmotif of the "Roar again of airplanes in the sky" whose pilots "are sweating and nervous at the controls in the hot cabins" (54). These bombers with their "loveless bombs" perform as a mobile umbrella shadowing both the giggling girls, "all pretty/every-whichway," and the crippled lady, who "explains French grammar with a loud sweet voice:/ Regarder is to look."

Looking is the genius of this poem, and it is not only the "scatological insight" [11] that Ginsberg's eye exploits as he observes the "pelvic energy" of the crippled girl's bouncing body, but it is the deeper vision of the "unseen" being "proved by the seen." Professor Hart, "enlightened by the years," walks "through the doorway and arcade he built (in his mind)/and knows—he too saw the ruins of Yucatan once—" (56). The unseen which the poet reveals through his perception surely is the sense of community that binds all mankind together: ". . . we all look up," Ginsberg observes, "silence moves, huge changes upon the ground, and in the air thoughts fly all over filling space" (58).

The salutary moment is both spiritual and poetic. "My grief at Peter's not loving me was grief at not loving myself," the poet unconcludes. Minds that are broken in "beautiful bodies [are] unable to receive love because not knowing the self as lovely." The illumination is no less poignant because it derives from Whitman. Indeed, from Whitman the poetic impulse behind the creation becomes much clearer; for, in the words of the "True American," Walt Whitman, Ginsberg's literary foundation can be seen: "I know I am solid and sound/To me the converging objects of the universe perpetually flow,/All are written to me, and I must get what the writing means." [12]

III *Love and Nakedness*

The doctrine of "nakedness" that Ginsberg continually preaches is implicit in "Sather Gate Illumination"; and it, too, owes much to Whitman. "Undrape! you are not guilty to me, nor stale nor discard," one reads in "Song of Myself": "I see through the broadcloth and gingham whether or no,/And am around, tenacious, acquisitive, tireless, and cannot/be shaken away." [13] Clothes are not only a hindrance to lovemaking; they are the garments of illusion with which men shamefully hide their humanity. Mind, too often, is the grim tailor, which appears to be one of the underlying themes of "Love Poem on Theme by Whitman" (41). In this poem, the poet shares the nuptial bed of "the bridegroom and the bride" of humanity whose "bodies fallen from heaven stretched out waiting naked and restless" are open to his physical visitation. As he buries his face "in their shoulders and breasts, breathing their skin . . . bodies locked shuddering naked, hot lips and buttocks screwed into each other," he hears the "bride cry for forgiveness" and the groom "covered with tears of passion and compassion." What is described so sensually is an orgasm of community—a nude coming together of primal human hearts from which the poet rises "up from the bed replenished with last intimate gestures and kisses of farewell."

The graphic extremity to which the erotic description takes one is an all-out blitzkrieg against shame. The bed is a possible world of contracted time and space—the identical bed threatened by the "busy old fool, unruly Sunne" that John Donne so beautifully has celebrated.[14] In Ginsberg's poem, however, it is not the "Sunne" which is the intruding landlady of this secret tryst but the mind. Once again, the "cold touch of philosophy" withers primordial love. The conclusion of Ginsberg's poem drops an ironic veil between love and life as it is lived. Shameless physical love occurs

> all before the mind awakes, behind shades and closed
> doors in a darkened house where inhabitants roam
> unsatisfied in the night, nude ghosts seeking each
> other out in the silence.

Some of the pathos of Ginsberg's personal attempts to revive "nude ghosts" can be appreciated in his mock-heroic epic, "The Green Automobile" (11–16), a visionary, yet autobiographical excursion with Neal Cassidy to Denver, where the two latter-day cavaliers seek to

> . . . be the angels of the world's desire
> and take the world to bed with us before
> we die.

Sleeping alone, or with companion,
girl or fairy sheep or dream,
I'll fail of lacklove, you, satiety:
all men fall, our fathers fell before. . . . (15)

Love is the prize, the holy grail, of these deprived wanderers, and the urgent necessity of drinking from this universal cup erases hetero- and homosexual boundaries. "*Malest Cornifici Tuo Catullo*" (47) is just one of Ginsberg's several poetic, homosexual confessions; and few can deny the poignancy of its brief, candid apology:

Ah don't think I'm sickening.
You're angry at me. For all of my lovers?
It's hard to eat shit, without having visions;
when they have eyes for me it's like Heaven.

IV *The* Ubi Sunt

One of the universals of poetic expression is the mood which remembrance of things past evokes. The modern "*Ubi sunt*" sometimes arouses a poignancy that rivals even the most powerful of the Old English lyrics. The subject is the same: alienation; the mood, however, is more personal because the bygone times are less distant and the feelings are closer to man's sense of how rapidly the ravages of time close in upon him. "The Wanderer" and "The Seafarer" give a taste of the loneliness of the unaccommodated *scop,* bereft of his mead hall and the comfort of his protecting thane. Modern mead halls lack the magnificence of Heorot; "matter is water" (72) the twentieth-century singer must confess. And so the heavy nostalgia of an Anglo-Saxon heritage must be translated into faster tempos and tawdrier, less localized scenes. The universal feeling has not changed, but the props are demythologized. The result is a poem such as " 'Back on Times Square Dreaming of Times Square' " (70–71).

The conflict of this poem is measured by the collision of actuality with memory. The medium is place—Times Square—and the kinetic throwoff of the poem is the sad contrast of what *is* with what *was.* Times Square, a "memorial of ten years," is now emotionally neutralized by the imposing facticity of "the green &

grooking McGraw/Hill offices" (70). A "sad trumpeter" is petitioned to "stand on the empty streets at dawn/and blow a silver chorus to the buildings of Times Square"; but obviously the time for silver choruses is long past—ten years past—and what music now exists belongs to a solitary cop walking by who is "invisible with his music."

Surprisingly, the contrast is not traditional; that is, present loneliness versus past joy. The contrast is between two distinct types of loneliness which superimpose one quality of alienation with a deeper tint of the same. The polar symbols are the McGraw-Hill offices of the present moment and the "Globe Hotel" of memory. Both poles share a grimness which the fine discrimination of the poet separates with the subtle reminiscence. "I was lonely," he confesses, just as he implicitly avows his present loneliness. The modern mead hall ("The Globe Hotel") boasted little of the comfort and solace of its historical antecedents, for it was a place where "Garver lay in

> grey beds there and hunched his
> back and cleaned his needles—
> where I lay many nights on the nod
> from his leftover bloody cottons
> and dreamed of Blake's voice talking. . . . (70)

Returning to this place is acknowledging the quickened pace of mutability: "Garver's dead in Mexico two years, hotel's vanished into a parking lot/And I'm back here—sitting on the streets/again" (70).

The "*Ubi Sunt*" lament which speaks through this poem is the forlorn query: Where are the not-so-good old days before mass media raped man's special mission? It is a lament to the stolen Beat Generation—an attitude that was popularized to extinction:

> The movies took our language, the
> great red signs
> A DOUBLE BILL OF GASSERS
> Teen Age Nightmare
> Hooligans of the Moon. (70)

Underlying the lament is the apologetic protest of misrepresentation:

> But we were never nightmare
> hooligans but seekers of
> the blond nose for Truth. (71)

The theme, then, of this poem is missionary martyrdom. From the ashes of an apparently defeated memory arises the poet's conviction about the prophetic validity of what had once occurred. "We are legend," he concedes, "invisible but legendary, as prophecied" (71).

The next poem, "My Sad Self" (72), is less protestant, less prophetic. It is difficult to defend much of this poem from the charge of "crude sentimentality" which the *Times Literary Supplement* insists "is of a piece with the equally crude rhetoric, the hamfisted philosophizing, and the wholesale misuse of imagist and neosurrealist techniques" which pervade *Reality Sandwiches.*[15] This poem is a sentimental one, but it is somewhat superior to "Tears" (63) which is indeed an example of Ginsberg's apparent "belief that an emotion stated is an emotion conveyed."[16] "My Sad Self" baldly states an emotion: sadness; and this emotion is presented more or less as a premise as the poet gazes at New York from the top of the RCA Building. From this vantage point he catalogues various places, each with its attendant nostalgia ("my history summed up, my absences/and ecstasies in Harlem"). The universalizing lever in this poem—the device that lifts it from pure nostalgic sentimentality—is the concept of transiency that is suggested in the final lines of the first stanza:

> —sun shining down on all I own
> in one eyeblink to the horizon
> in my last eternity—
> matter is water.

Ginsberg owns all he sees because of his subjective relation to it ("Who digs Los Angeles IS Los Angeles!" [H, 21]). The natural corollary to this stance is the intransigence of things: "matter is water" (72).

The remainder of "My Sad Self" is a meandering journey through New York with the usual Ginsbergian reactions to the things he sees about him. For example, he stares "into all man's/plateglass, faces,/questioning after who loves . . ." (72); and, near the end of the poem, he unleashes his prophetic voice and painfully observes that "this graveyard . . . once seen/never regained or desired/in the mind to come . . . must disappear" (74).

V *Spontaneity and Meditation*

Norman MacCaig, who has admitted that "there's a great head of pressure built up in all that Allen Ginsberg writes," remarks that "the trouble is that often the fabric of the poem can't contain it—it explodes messily in your face, spattering you with gobbets and fragments of what may have been a fine body of experience." [17] This description seems an accurate one of

"FFFFF U U NN N
F U U N N N
FFFFF U U N N N
F U U N N N NY DEATH,"
F U U N NN
F UU N N

"I Beg You Come Back & Be Cheerful," "Aether," and several others. In these poems, "syntax is shot at sight, things are described in a catalogue of gasps, the light is lurid, distances enormous [and] . . . the wind blows from hysteria." [18] "Aether," perhaps, contains the justification for these excursions:

> Yet the experiments must continue!
> Every possible combination of Being—all
> the old ones! all the old Hindu
> Sabahadabadie-pluralic universes
> ringing in Grandiloquent
> Bearded Juxtaposition. . . . (84)

Many of these experiments were accomplished under the influence of various stimulants and drugs, but the literary significance is clear: the method is spontaneous dictation of experience without benefit of afterthought. Perhaps the typical reaction is, again, MacCaig's, whose summary is: "Terribly Romantic, in a diabolical sort of way. And tediously self-regarding. . . . It's the continuous pumping-up that I distrust." [19]

"Siesta in Xbalba," the best poem of *Reality Sandwiches,* is not "pumped up" at all; but, as James Scully feels, it "recalls . . . the quieter vision of Henry Vaughan."[20] What is reminiscent of Vaughan is control more than anything else. The reader is not asked to fill his mind with abstract eternities or chaotic meanderings of a turgid mind; instead, he finally has something tangible to deal with. Ginsberg presents in this poem a real, vibrant world to consider; and, at the same time, it is a world pregnant with intimations of immortality.

Like Vaughan's "The World" ("I saw Eternity last night . . ."), "Siesta in Xbalba" makes the effort for revelation:

> Late sun opening the book,
> blank page like light,
> invisible words unscrawled,
> impossible syntax
> of apocalypse—(21)

The poem even programs a method: "let the mind fall down" (21). From the very beginning of the poem, therefore, there is a yearning for an apocalyptic vision—a setting almost assured of producing the proper mystic mood—and, finally, a yielding up of the rational discipline so that the poet becomes almost pure receptor. What occurs in the poem from this point on is what George Poulet might describe as the "infinite receptivity" which is the genius of Walt Whitman's thought.[21] Ginsberg obviously enjoys the stance. He is in a hammock, suspended, so to speak, above the world and yet still of it, while white doves copulate underneath him (21) and monkeys bark. The reader is told that the poet has "succumbed to this temptation" of "doing nothing but lying in a hammock" (21); and he is prepared for observation and apocalyptic musing.

The musing initially takes place in the form of a dream flashback—"an eternal kodachrome" (22), Ginsberg calls it—where his friends at a party are frozen in his mind. Clearly, the idea is to present an *inauthentic* contrast to the *authentic* situation the poet is in at Xbalba because the people at the party are described as "posed together," with "stylized gestures" and "familiar visages." They are all, he concludes, "posturing in one frame,/superficially gay/or tragic as may be,/illumed with the fatal/character and intelligent/actions of their lives" (23).

Immediately following this dream flashback is a description of the poet's own pretentiously stark surroundings: "And I in a concrete room/above the abandoned/labyrinth of Palenque/measuring my fate,/wandering solitary in the wild/—blinking single-minded/at a bleak idea—" (23). Clearly, there is a note of superiority here. Friends are trivial, but "I" am serious is the note Ginsberg seems to strike; there is, of course, the usual cosmic trump card to be played: the oncoming mystic vision. Fatigued from gazing at the bleak idea, the poet awaits the moment when

> my soul might shatter
> at one primal moment's
> sensation of the vast
> movement of divinity. (23)

There is obviously an inchoate quest operating in the debris of the mind that has fallen down, and it seems to be directed toward the usual eternity which so often is the misty goal of Ginsberg's poems. The reason is probably the same as Whitman's: "Eternity gives similitude to all periods and locations and processes, and animates and inanimates forms, and . . . is the bond of time." [22] Such a valuable commodity as this bond is certainly worthy of the highest poetry, and it helps once again to explain Ginsberg's views concerning drugs. If eternity is the "bond of time"—the thing which glues everything together into community and permits everyone to be an angel—then it is reasonable that any access to this state would be well worth the price. Even without drugs the search for Eternity can be salutary:

> As I leaned against a tree
> inside the forest
> expiring of self-begotten love,
> I looked up at the stars absently,
> as if looking for
> something else in the blue night
> through the boughs,
> and for a moment saw myself
> leaning against a tree. . . . (23)

Time and eternity, as the glue that binds all things together, is developed as a concept later in the poem when Ginsberg meditates upon a death's-head. Part of his fascination with the death's-head is its relevance to the principle of prophecy. He is impressed by the fact that it "thinks its way/through centuries the thought of the same night in which I sit/in skully meditation" (26). Here is an instance of eternity indeed obliterating time but in the fashion of biblical prophecy. The anterior artisan, the maker of the death's-head, sculpted his artifact until it fully represented his idea; but now, Ginsberg muses, the death's-head communicates that idea across time:

> but now his fine thought's vaguer
> than my dream of him:
> and only the crude skull figurement's
> gaunt insensible glare is left. . . . (26)

The philosophical substratum of this small passage of the poem would seem to be the idea that truth (even history) is entirely subjective. Works of art, be they poems or death's-heads, have the capability of triggering or exciting thoughts in future individuals. The sense of oneness that eternity brings with it acts as a sort of guarantee of this phenomenon and presents the possibility of bridges across time. Real history, then, does not operate chronologically, logically, or rationally. History is apocalypse, so that Ginsberg can say:

> I alone know the great crystal door
> to the House of Night,
> a legend of centuries
> —I and a few indians. (29)

Any other access to history—any other solution to the "impossible syntax" of the hieroglyphics—cannot possibly yield what the death's-head potentially can surrender subjectively to the eternalized viewer. Unless the mind is allowed to "fall down," the rational apparatus will filter out the past:

> Time's slow wall overtopping
> all that firmament of mind,
> as if a shining waterfall of leaves and rain

were built down solid from the endless sky
through which no thought can pass. (28)

The first part of the poem ends with a rejection and a tentative affirmation: "There is a god/dying in America" (33) which is the institutionalized religious impulse. At the same time, there is also "an inner/anterior image/of divinity/beckoning me out/to pilgrimage" (33).

Part Two of this poem, "Return to the United States" (33), possesses a stark, generally crisp descriptive style and only one real intrusion of Ginsbergian metaphysics. The reader is told, finally, that "The problem is isolation" (36), a statement later followed by the lament: "What solitude I've finally inherited" (37). What these lines appear to mean is that Ginsberg has failed in a way. If what he hoped to retain from his night in Xbalba was a vision of Whitman's "vast similitude [which] interlocks all,/All spheres grown, ungrown, small, large, suns, moons, planets,/All distances of place however wide,/All distances of time . . . ,"[23] what he actually returned with was less ambitious: "a few Traditions,/ metrical, mystical, manly/ . . . and certain characteristic flaws" (38). The isolation, it would also seem, is not entirely his own; it's the isolation of the whole universe. The temptation for social criticism becomes too strong in the final lines, and the *real* loneliness and the *real* isolation are finally diagnosed as natural consequences of "The nation over the border [America]" which "grinds its arms and dreams of war" (39).

Intellectual sentimentality appears to be Ginsberg's Achilles' heel, and one reason for the success of "Siesta in Xbalba" is the fact that the thundering onslaughts upon God, upon eternity, upon the cosmos, and so on, are kept unusually under control. There is more attention to things in this poem than in most of the others, which anchors it to a refreshing empirical plane too often missing in the later work. An Oriental clarity in some places in the poem even brings metaphysics nearer to the reader's grasp, much in the way suggested in "Cézanne's Ports," for example. One such instance is the simple description of the night in the midst of the rain forest:

I can see the moon
moving over the edge of the night forest
and follow its destination

through the clear dimensions of the sky
from end to end of the dark
circular horizon. (25)

If nothing else, the idea in this short excerpt is *rendered* rather than garrulously bellowed. It is structural, not strident; and the quiet control of "Siesta in Xbalba" is a welcome reminder that the best poems are most often made rather than notated.

VI *Assessment*

It is very difficult to assess *Reality Sandwiches* as a whole because the book, which spans seven years of poetic development, modestly claims to be merely "scribbled secret notebooks, and wild typewritten pages, for yr [*sic*] own joy." It would be silly to pretend that many of the poems are not simply amateurish, pretentious, clumsy, and, at times, even downright dull. One bittersweet reviewer of the *Times Literary Supplement* has conceded that "in among this amateurish material . . . there are moments of real excitement, and poems which are firmly restrained and delicately balanced. There are not many, but there are enough to give one hope for Mr. Ginsberg's future development."[24] The assessment is probably true, but what the reviewer hopefully regards as signs of "future development" are perhaps more accurately carry-overs from Ginsberg's less flamboyant earlier versifying. Ginsberg is not working *toward* what would be considered traditional control; he is fleeing from it as rapidly as possible.

One is left, then, with the kind of response to which James Scully invariably resorts when he reviews Ginsberg's work: Scully finds Ginsberg's worth in his "sense of humanity." The phrase is ambiguous and slippery, and even Scully's attempt to clarify does no more than suggest the type of power that he finds in the poems. Nevertheless, according to Scully this sense of humanity is Ginsberg's attempt "to uncover a community";[25] and such attempts have perfectly respectable credentials. Walt Whitman, for example, was doing the very same thing when he wrote:

Divine am I inside and out, and I make holy whatever I touch
or am touched from,

> The scent of these arm-pits aroma finer than prayer,
> This head more than churches, bibles, and all creeds.[26]

In a way, Whitman's liturgy of the divine, human self appears to be the one constant, yet elusive, goal toward which Ginsberg has been striving throughout most of his career. One form of its progress appears in "Sather Gate Illumination," where the final lines declare that "Who loves himself loves me who love myself" (58); but the fullest expression in a poem more recent than any in *Reality Sandwiches,* is in "The Change." [27]

VII *"The Change"*

"The Change" is a pivotal poem for Ginsberg. He considers it a testimony of a complete reversal in his thinking which drew his concentration away from expanding the consciousness toward plunging into his heart. In essence, the experience that "The Change" documents was a crisis that resolved the mind-body conflict for Ginsberg. So important was it for him that he describes his return from Asia in 1963, after this experience, as complete bankruptcy. "My energies of the last . . . oh, 1948 to 1963, all completely washed up," he says of it in his *Paris Review* interview.[28] What happened during the Asian trip that could have affected him so decisively?

For one thing, prior to the trip Ginsberg had, as he puts it, painted himself into a corner with drugs. Although taking drugs made him nauseous, he continued to take them, not, it appears, because of addiction so much as because he felt he was "duly bound and obliged for the sake of consciousness expansion . . . and seeking more direct contact with primate sensation, nature, to continue." [29] Part of the problem was an identity crisis. Drug-induced hallucinations had made him question the validity of his own identity, not to mention his fear of being literally melted into the universe. The portion of Ginsberg's letter to William Burroughs, mentioned before, describing his experience with *Yage* reveals the magnitude of his preoccupation with self and death under the influence of these powerful drugs.[30] Later he describes the subject of his hallucination as "a Being whose presence I had not yet fully sensed." [31]

What worried Ginsberg at this point was the question of authentic reality—whether his vision was real or his normal consciousness. Burroughs' reply to Ginsberg's appeal for consolation is interesting: "Your AYUASKA consciousness is more valid than 'Normal Consciousness'? Whose 'Normal Consciousness'?" [32] Ginsberg was under great pressure to continue his exploration into the non-human dimensions of consciousness. His feeling was that he should "not be afraid of death but go into death. Go into the non-human, go into the cosmic so to speak; that God was death, and if I wanted to attain God I had to die. . . . So I thought that what I was put up to was to therefore break out of my body, if I wanted to attain complete consciousness." [33]

The Asian trip helped to resolve this problem at least partially. Swami Shivananda told him, "Your own heart is your guru"; and, after a little thought, it occurred to Ginsberg that "it was the heart that I was seeking. In other words it wasn't consciousness, it wasn't *petites sensations*, sensation defined as expansion of mental consciousness to include more data . . . the area that I was seeking was the heart rather than the mind." [34] The implications of this realization were enormous because it meant renouncing virtually all of his previous suppositions; it even meant renouncing Blake. "The Change" is, therefore, a document of a crucial turning point in a man's life. "I was suddenly free to love myself again," says Ginsberg, "and therefore love the people around me, in the form that they already were. And love myself in my own form as I am." [35]

Dramatic as sudden conversions are, particularly when rendered poetically, it is difficult to see in this one a decisive enough change from previous thinking. There appears to be a bit of Romantic "pumping-up" about the whole experience on Kyoto-Tokyo Express because the principles that evolve from it are nearly identical with those avowed in much earlier poems. "Sather Gate Illumination" is the most obvious example. One explanation for what appears to be an inconsistency is the underlying presence of Walt Whitman in so much of Ginsberg's work. After much of the *Sturm und Drang*, the visions, and the drugs are stripped away from Ginsberg's poetry, what remains is usually "Old graybeard," Walt Whitman, in somewhat diluted form. One may compare, for example, the following excerpts, the first from "Song of Myself," the second from "The Change":

All truths wait in all things
They neither hasten their own delivery nor resist it,
They do not need the obstetric forceps of the surgeon,
The insignificant is as big to me as any
(What is less or more than a touch?).[36]

. . . .

In this dream I am the Dreamer
 and the Dreamed I am
 that I am Ah but I have
 always known

oooh for the hate I have spent
 in denying my image & cursing
 the breasts of illusion—[37]

It seems fairly obvious that Ginsberg has acquiesced to a position that he has "always known" in this stanza—a stance which once again recognizes that ideas ultimately reside in things, just as Whitman and William Carlos Williams had counseled him in the beginning. Ginsberg adds the final ironic comment on his change in language that could easily be Dr. Williams':

> In order to get back to now, in order to get back to the total awareness of now and contact, sense perception contact with what was going on around me, or direct vision of the moment, now I'd have to give up this continual churning thought process of yearning back to a visionary state. It's all very complicated. And idiotic.[38]

The poem itself is not remarkable, and the reader can be very easily put off by its incessant egocentricity and somewhat precious scatterings of Far Eastern myth and lore (Ginsberg himself supplied notes for some of the more exotic images; these remind one of a recently returned traveler adding comments to his color slides). The message is quite clearly delivered in several succinct ways:

Close the portals of the festival?
Open the portals to what is . . .

or,

I am that I am—
    Closed off from this
The schemes begin, roulette,
    brainwaves, bony dice,
    Stereoscopic motorcycles
    Stroboscopes and Scaly
        Serpents winding thru
            cloud spaces of
                What is not—

Many of the comments begin to sound like testimonials from "mystics anonymous":

I am that I am I am the
    man & the Adam of hair in
    my loins. This is my spirit and
    physical shape I inhabit
    this Universe Oh weeping
    against what is my
    own nature for now

The point of the poem is simple and repetitive: no more visions; live in the skin and the present tense.

VIII Wichita Vortex Sutra

The poems of Ginsberg after "The Change" seem to become more and more politically and socially concerned—perhaps as a natural consequence of his giving up the visions. He even wrote what might be considered an occasional poem in 1965 in honor of his being crowned the King of May: "*Kral Majales.*" [39] The long, clanky line appears in this poem, and there is the usual frank scatology. Remnants of Indian religious mythology appear like postcards tucked away in the bottom of old valises, but there is also a concern for what is happening today in the world of men that is somehow a pleasant relief from the former self-indulgent quests for self-knowledge. And the new spirit of "telling it like it is" of these later poems no doubt serves to endear Ginsberg to the younger generation.

The poem opens with criticism of Communists and capitalists, both of whom in various ways bring intolerable pressures upon "the Just man." The logic of the attack becomes a bit clearer when it is explained later in the poem that Ginsberg was "arrested thrice in Prague." The series of indignities that occur to him in the course of these arrests are documented before finally being atoned for by his being crowned the King of May. *Kral Majales* soon takes on a symbolic significance; it represents "the power of sexual youth," "industry in eloquence," "action in amour," and "old Human poesy." Ginsberg has been chosen King of May because he "heard the voice of Blake in a vision,/and repeat[s] that voice," because he "sleeps with teenagers laughing," because he "may be expelled from my Kingdom with honor, as of old,/To shew the difference between Caesar's Kingdom and the Kingdom of the May of Man." The last reason seems to be the most comprehensive; it embraces the usual "we-feel-and-love-one-another-versus you calculate-and-brutalize-humanity attitude of hipdom."

The rest of the poem is a rather eclectic catalogue of sights, sounds, and random thoughts that occur to Ginsberg en route to London. There seems to be no particular pattern to the observations; one of them, in fact, seems pure mawkish sentimentality:

> And I am the King of May because I touched my finger to
> my forehead saluting
> a luminous heavy girl with trembling hands who said "one
> moment Mr Ginsberg"
> before a fat young Plainclothesman stepped between our
> bodies . . .

A poem that is more recent (1966) and has something more concrete to say is *Wichita Vortex Sutra.*[40] A long piece (fifteen pages), it seems to be patterned after several other forms. William Carlos Williams' *Paterson* has certainly been influential in terms of the structure, and the sensation of being swept into the vortex of some kind of American linguistic hell reminds one of Dante. If there is such a thing as "anti-poetic," this poem might qualify on the grounds that it spills over into television commercials, newspaper headlines, radio disk-jockey patter, news broadcasts, neon signs—in short, all the semantic flotsam and jetsam that has inundated American life.

There are several subjects in the poem. The Vietnam war appears on the surface to be the overriding concern, but as the reader is swept closer and closer to the vortex of consternation, it soon becomes apparent that the war is merely a symptom of something even more basic: the elemental violence of humanity. As with most calamitous things, they have their beginnings in trivia; and Ginsberg finds the genesis of American violence (the vortex) not only in Wichita (midcenter U.S.A.) but a particular building in Wichita: The Hotel Eaton; for

> Carrie Nation began the war on Vietnam here
> with an angry smashing axe
> attacking Wine
> Here fifty years ago, by her violence
> began a vortex of hatred that defoliated the Mekong Delta—
> (14)

One message of the poem is the contagion of violence that has spread across the breadth of America and that has even been exported overseas. A second message is about language. As Ginsberg conceives language in this poem, it is magic power. It can provide "Black Magic language, formulas for reality," or it can reflect the sameness of hearts in all humans, at which time it merits the name "prophecy." Prophecy is equivalent to truth; "formulas for reality" are deceptions, disguised lies, "bad guesses," and all the paraphernalia that comes between what really happens and one's apprehension of it. Obviously, all the news media are providing mere "formulas for reality":

> Has anyone looked in the eyes of the wounded?
> Have we seen but paper faces, Life Magazine?
> Are screaming faces made of dots,
> electric dots on Television. . . . (3)

Wichita Vortex Sutra is really a poem about "how to speak the right language" (9); it is also a lament over the "Sorcerer's Apprentice who lost control/of the simplest broomstick in the world:/Language" (5). The apprentice is the administration who is responsible for the fact that "almost all our language has been taxed by war" (9). The evidence comes blaring through the car radio as Ginsberg speeds across the Midwest plains, and it screams from the front pages of the *Lincoln Star,* the *Albuquer-*

que Journal and "NBCBSUPAPINSLIFE." The heinousness of the situation is that "all this black language [is] writ by machine!" (8).

The antidote for this sick language is a familiar prescription: prophecy. Prophecy is based upon the fact that "All we do is for this frightened thing/we call Love" and that "spoken lonesomeness is Prophecy" (9). The power potential of prophecy is simply that it is the most fundamental communication between humans; it assumes that the hearts of a Vietnamese and an American are the same. It acknowledges

> that the rest of the earth is unseen
> the outer universe invisible,
> Unknown except thru
> language
> airprint
> magic images
> or prophecy of the secret
> heart the same
> in Waterville as Saigon one human form:
> When a woman's heart bursts in Waterville
> a woman screams equal in Hanoi—(8)

The poem gains in intensity as it nears the climax: the arrival at Wichita. Ginsberg manages to build a structural suspense through his usual strategy of cumulative images. In this case, the cataloguing is almost entirely from communications media and commercial ideograms ("Supermarket Texaco brilliance . . . ," "Ooh! sensitive city lights of Hamburger & Skelley's Gas . . . ," etc.); but the sheer energy that is released somehow makes the fantastic conclusion of the poem seem almost credible:

> Proud Wichita! vain Wichita
> cast the first stone!—
> that murdered my mother
> who died of the communist anticommunist psychosis
> in the madhouse one decade long ago . . . (14)

What the reader is left with in these recent poems is brute poetic power that presumes to bulldoze a specific passion into a listener's consciousness. Whether or not such quantitative rhetoric adds up to what a consensus would consider poetry is probably a subject for unresolvable debate. At any rate, a pattern of sorts does emerge from Ginsberg's progression through the years; roughly, that pattern can be described as a journey from controlled, structural rendering of a poem to passionate, spontaneous prophesying. Certainly, the urge to prophesy begets an urgent feeling; but art demands that feeling be restrained at least to the limits of intelligibility. To quote Karl Shapiro again, "When the poet feels that he is experiencing history or the universe, you may be sure he is about to make a fool of himself." [41] This point is to be pondered.

CHAPTER 7

Envoi

THERE is nothing revolutionary about Kenneth Rexroth's view that "the problem of poetry is the problem of communication itself." [1] With modern writers, however, the problem thickens because they want to communicate so badly. Paul O'Neil, for instance, feels that Allen Ginsberg "communicates excitement like a voice yelling from inside a police car";[2] and with this simple assertion he manages to gather up most of the major issues about the prophet-poet: (1) his exciting energy; (2) his protestant attitude toward institutions and authority; and (3) his fundamental oracular stance—he yells. To these three characteristics one should also add his penchant for prophecy, his Surrealism, and his mysticism; but these are merely problematical confabulations of the basic Ginsberg style, and the essentials of Ginsberg's poetic identity are rather nicely gathered up in O'Neil's colorful image.

To communicate excitement, however, is in itself neither a particularly difficult nor an ennobling task—particularly for one who has no scruples about shedding his clothes at a public poetry reading. The beneficence of communicating excitement hinges upon the sort of excitement being communicated. In poetry, presumably, this excitement almost always involves the questions of art, nature, or both. In other words, the human imagination can be poetically gratified by imitations of nature, by esthetic distortions of nature which yield literary items which one classifies as beautiful, or by the traditional combination of the two: poetry which simultaneously teaches and pleases (combines *sentence* and *solas*).

It is very difficult to classify Ginsberg's work as a whole under any one of these three labels. Theoretically, in conversation, Ginsberg tends to speak like his friend Jack Kerouac who represents the extreme position of imitation of nature. Ginsberg always seems ready to leap to the defense of Kerouac's "Spontaneous Prose," and his own disregard for syntax, spelling, and punctuation seems to confirm his allegiance to this point of view. Nature, in this case, would be defined by both Ginsberg and Kerouac as whatever happens to them in thought or deed. A more comprehensive way of describing their attitude might be to say that they are interested in making the real more real. This description seems to be a workable premise for looking at Ginsberg's poetry until one runs head-on into his drug-induced Surrealistic productions, and then the problem becomes complicated by the consideration of whether drugs or trances serve to make the real more—or less—real. At once the problem ceases to be the concern of literature and becomes one for psychologists and biochemists. If one insists on keeping the situation in the purview of literature (as Ginsberg forces one to do), one must expand the definitions of reality to include all subjective occurrences and legitimize hallucination as a viable access to an inward reality.

Several considerations must immediately be brought in at this point. First, there is the very common-sense view of Karl Shapiro who insists that "poetic knowledge is not a leaping to the unknown; on the contrary, it is a painful engagement with the known." [3] Shapiro would include as part of "leaping to the unknown" such things as trances, Surrealism in almost any form, mysticism, and prophecy. The position he represents, therefore, is that of the poetic purist: the man who wants poets to write poetry, philosophers to write philosophy, and prophets to write prophecy; for any mixing of these functions dilutes their potency into amateurishness. While there is much that Shapiro admires about Ginsberg, it is obvious that he would find large portions of Ginsberg's work reprehensible for the above reasons.

A second consideration that must be quickly interjected is that of the modern passion for obliterating artifice in order to penetrate deeper into life—again a variation on the Kerouac credo of "Spontaneous Prose." This attitude assumes that creation is corruption; that to make deliberately and consciously is to destroy the naturalness of the subject. Ginsberg, again, seems to fit into this pattern. Shapiro's reply to the position provides some common-sense anchorage: "Human experience is chaotic, but human experience in art is orderly." [4]

The problem, then, falls quite simply into the age-old controversy between nature and art. Ginsberg and a good portion of his milieu understand artifice in terms almost unintelligible to the orthodox establishment. Artifice, to them, is emotionally based. It is manipulating the physiology of the human body in order to achieve the elusive more-real real rather than depending upon a cerebral "engagement with the known." In short, experience is king—and the more intense the experience, the more exciting the communication of it.

The ease with which a reverence for experience generates a religious attitude toward existence is only too familiar. The obsession of early Puritan ancestors for inward testimony of their salvation is only one example of an endless chain of connections between religion and experience. Friedrich Schleiermacher, Rudolph Otto, and William James offer overwhelming evidence of this simple claim; and it is not at all surprising that Ginsberg, Kerouac, Snyder, and a host of other new American writers should be vitally concerned with religious experience. With Ginsberg, however, the religious quest has become so intense as to obscure his poetry. In too many cases he has crossed the vocational line between poetry and prophecy—and compromised his potency. When Ginsberg runs beyond the natural poetic boundary lines, even his most sympathetic admirers frown. While egotism is the privilege of the poet, prophesying tends to smother him in a mire of self-delusion; the potent query that stares one in the face is simply: Does this sort of presumption have any place in modern poetry?

Obviously, such a question is unanswerable. Poetry is not yet a science; and one is finally left with the irrevocable wisdom of Sir John Rothenstein, the former director of the Tate Gallery: "Art derives from the intention of the artist. But time is the only impeccable judge." [5] But what are the intentions of Allen Ginsberg? It is fairly obvious to the general reader and to many critics that a great deal of Ginsberg's work is sloppy sentimentality posing as profundity or honesty. At times the amateurishness cannot even claim honesty; for, as Thomas Parkinson has observed, "Allen Ginsberg's public posture on literary matters is that of an innocent who writes from impulse, but he knows better." [6] Indeed, Ginsberg *does* know better; and this knowledge raises the question once again of what he is about: Does he want to be a poet? Or is he more interested in being a prophet? Reviewers have had a field day castigating his work when he has attempted to be both, and even his own camp occasionally must blow the whistle on some of his excesses.

Part of the continual pressure upon Ginsberg to be other than a poet comes from the fact that he has come to "stand for" something in American life. What he stands for is disturbing to most people, irritating to others, baffling to the hopelessly "square," and provocatively significant to serious thinkers about the problems of modern existence. Harvey Cox, author of *The Secular City*, is only one of thousands of theologians, professors, sociologists, and politicians who unabashedly regard Ginsberg as a representative of a point of view which, if it is not altogether correct, is at least healthy to the disturbed social scene of today. Cox, who calls Ginsberg "the elder statesman of one of the most significant subcultures in American society," considers him theologically important enough to publish an "Open Letter" to him in *Commonweal*.[7] The gist of the letter is by way of a salute. "Maybe you and your shocking friends are reminding us," writes Cox, "of something about Christianity we'd almost forgotten, the rhythm of dropping out, listening and then dropping back in."

The vital question from a literary angle is: Can the "elder statesman of a significant subculture" find happiness as a mere poet? Was Kenneth Rexroth a prophet in his own right when he said in 1957 that Ginsberg runs the risk of turning into a popular entertainer? [8] The answer seems to be that Ginsberg has chosen not to be a *mere* poet. Unfortunately, he has presumed to be more; and it is this "more" that has caused him so much trouble with the mass media, the critics, the authorities, and, most importantly, his own poetry. A typical review of a Ginsberg poetry volume suggests the truth of this assertion. James Dickey, for example, after stating that "Ginsberg's writings are of the familiar our-love-against-their-madness-and-money variety," then observes that "everyone in Ginsberg's book [*Howl*, in this case] is hopped up on benzedrine, reefers, or whiskey, and is doing something as violently and loudly as he can, in 'protest' or 'fulfillment.' What emerges from all this is an Attitude, since most of the writing itself is in no sense distinctive." [9]

It is invariably "the Attitude" of Ginsberg that attracts more attention than the poetry; and, while it can be safely said that Ginsberg brings a lot of this upon himself, the misplaced attention is unfair both to criticism and to poetry. The problem, then, is to somehow make a workable separation between "the Attitude" and the poetry. This is not to say that poetic content and poetic form can be that neatly separated; they cannot—particularly in Ginsberg's case. What must be done is to recognize "the Attitude," appreciate its stance, and then judge the poetry as poetry. This statement simply says in another way what John Sisk has averred: that literature such as Ginsberg's engages in a dialectic tension with social conservatism and that "such an engagement would assume that the Beat writers merit no preferred treatment simply because of their tradition-sanctioned subversiveness; and it would assume that they must prove themselves as writers and not expect to get by on novelty, shock-effect or sublime intentions." [10]

After the novelty, shock, and sublime intentions have been brushed aside from Ginsberg's work, what is left? To listen to the serious, sympathetic critics one word can be heard consistently—*energy*. This assessment is a briefer, less colorful statement of what O'Neil meant when he spoke of Ginsberg's ability to "communicate excitement like a voice yelling from inside a police car"; but both assertions coincide perfectly with Charles Olson's definition of a poem: ". . . the poem itself must, at all points, be a high energy-construct and, at all points, an energy discharge." [11]

From the point of view of energy, then, what can be said about Ginsberg's poetry? Ginsberg achieves energy in his poetry through two modes: the tightness of his catalogues and his meter. To deal with the first method, it can be said that his success stems from his ability to select potent images and to connect them in a fashion that accords with Olson's counsel that "ONE PERCEPTION MUST IMMEDIATELY AND DIRECTLY LEAD TO A FURTHER PERCEPTION." [12] Speed, as well as selection of images, is certainly a factor; but even more important as far as Ginsberg is concerned is the fact that, when he deals with concrete images as in *Howl* and *Kaddish*, the effect is more poetically pungent than when he makes his narcotic assaults upon the unknown ("Aether," for example).

When Ginsberg surrenders to his abstractions the consequences are usually Surrealistic disaster. Although his intentions may be equally sincere when he works with a physical object or a hallucination, the respective results prove the pudding. The case is put well by Karl Shapiro: ". . . surrealism tries to break down all barriers between the subject and object and to produce a delirium of reality. But this delirium is as artificial as an invented dream, lacking both spontaneity and selectivity. Surrealism is one of the more advanced forms of public speech and it is popular with the poet who is most interested in translating dogma into sensation." [13] As poet and prophet, it would be difficult to release Ginsberg from the charge of "translating dogma into sensation." This ability is his stock-in-trade; and, even though he possesses a certain Whitmanesque expertise in producing what Ciardi calls the "tight catalogue," this quality does not compensate for the fact that he is clearly not in Isaiah's league.

The second source of Ginsberg's energy is his meter, which is a consideration closely aligned with vocal utterance. Thomas Parkinson cogently devotes a good deal of consideration to "the importance of oral delivery and the writer's physical dramatic presence to the full impact of the poetry of Ginsberg and Ferlinghetti." Essentially, Parkinson's point is that the syntactical violations, the lack of punctuation, grammar, proper spelling, and so forth are attempts to "shift from conventional idiom to actual, to increase the vocality of the verse." [14] Of course, he is correct; and one must constantly remind himself that to read a Ginsberg poem is to read a score.

Aside from the vocal aspect of meter, one has Ginsberg's own description of his metrical method: "Hebraic-Melvillean bardic breath." There is no need to go into an explanation of what he means; it has been covered before. What is important, however, is Ginsberg's confidence that there is, to quote L. S. Dembo, a "kind of communication that, related to a mystical life force, transcends conventional language in the same way that music 'transcends' words." Dembo is speaking of Robert Duncan at this point, but he later makes the application to Ginsberg. "Important," Dembo continues, "is the assumption of an elemental sound or rhythm, prior to the language of significance, and quintessential to what is taken to be true poetry." [15] Those who have attended a poetry reading by Ginsberg are familiar with his technique of beginning each performance with an Indian chant:

Shiki Fu I Ku Ku Fu Shiki
Shiki Soku Ze Ku Ku Soku
Ze Shiki [16]

The logic behind this "elemental sound or rhythm" is that rhythm itself is not only a communication but a language of itself; there is a linguistic primitivism about the notion that places metrics far in the forefront of poetic concern. Dembo goes so far as to say that "it is precisely this notion of a rhythm, 'transconceptual and non-verbal,' that provides one of the main lines of continuity between the beat as individual, the beat as poet, and the beat as mystic. . . . As it appears in Beat poetry, the rhythm mystique is the extreme primitivistic extension of linguistic romanticism." [17]

If pure rhythmic energy connects the "Beat" individual, the Beat poet, and Beat mystic, it makes it all the harder to predict that Allen Ginsberg will probably not be remembered a century hence as anything but an obscure phenomenon of the 1950's and 1960's. The fault is not a lack of poetic talent on his part; it is rather that he will never be content to be mortal. He is like Rimbaud who wrote to his friend Paul Demeney:

> The poet makes himself a *seer* through a long, a prodigious and rational disordering of *all* the senses. Every form of love, of suffering, of madness; he searches himself, he consumes all the poisons in him, keeping only their quintessences. . . . He arrives at the unknown: and even if, half-crazed in the end, he loses the understanding of his visions, he has seen them! Let him croak in his leap into those unutterable and innumerable things: there will come other horrible workers: they will begin at the horizons where he has succumbed.[18]

With this attitude toward his existence, it is no wonder Ginsberg wrote in 1958:

> We are legend, invisible but
> legendary, as prophecied.[19]

Notes and References

Chapter One

1. *Empty Mirror* (New York, 1961), p. 7.
2. Jack Kerouac, "The Origins of the Beat Generation," *Playboy,* VI, 6 (June, 1959), 32.
3. John Ciardi, "Epitaph for the Dead Beats," *Saturday Review* (February 6, 1960), 11.
4. Dorothy Van Ghent, "Comment," *The Wagner Literary Magazine* (Spring, 1959), 27.
5. *Howl and Other Poems* (San Francisco, 1956), p. 8.
6. Herbert Gold, "The Beat Mystique," *Playboy,* (February, 1958), 87.
7. Norman Podhoretz, "The Know-nothing Bohemians," *Partisan Review,* XXV (Spring, 1958), 318.
8. Gregory Corso, "Variations on a Generation," *Gemini,* II (Spring, 1959), 49.
9. Norman Mailer, "The White Negro," *Dissent* (Summer, 1957). Reprinted in *Protest,* ed. Gene Feldman and Max Gartenberg (London: Panther, 1960), 289.
10. Paul O'Neil, "The Only Rebellion Around," *Life* (November 30, 1959), 123.
11. Sidney Cohen, *The Beyond Within: The LSD Story* (New York 1964).
12. Quoted in Alan W. Watts, *Beat Zen, Square Zen, and Zen* (San Francisco, 1959), p. 22. From *Marriage of Heaven and Hell,* "Proverbs of Hell."
13. June Bingham, "The Intelligent Square's Guide to Hippieland," *The New York Times Magazine* (September 25, 1967), 68.
14. John P. Sisk, "Beatniks and Tradition," *The Commonweal* (April 17, 1959), 76.
15. Paul O'Neil, *op. cit.,* 115.
16. "The Art of Poetry VIII," *The Paris Review,* 37 (Spring, 1966), 68.

17. Carl Michalson, "What Is Existentialism?" *Christianity and the Existentialists,* ed. Carl Michalson (New York, 1956), p. 13.
18. "The Art of Poetry VIII," *op. cit.,* 42–43.
19. John Clellan Holmes, "The Philosophy of the Beat Generation," *The Beats,* ed. Seymour Krim (Greenwich, Conn., 1960), p. 22.
20. Norman Mailer, "The White Negro," *op. cit.* (above, note 9), 289.
21. *Ibid.*
22. Carl Michalson, "What Is Existentialism?" *op. cit.,* p. 17.
23. *Ibid.,* p. 11.
24. Fantasy 7004, 1959. Reprinted in *The New American Poetry,* ed. Donald M. Allen (New York and London, 1960), pp. 412–13.
25. Jack Kerouac, "The Origins of the Beat Generation," *op. cit.,* 32.
26. Gary Snyder, "Note on the Religious Tendencies," *Liberation,* IV (June, 1959), 11.
27. "Footnote to *Howl,*" *Howl,* p. 21.
28. Kerouac, "The Origins of the Beat Generation," *op. cit.,* 42.
29. "The Art of Poetry VIII," *op. cit.,* 36–37.
30. Friedrich Schleiermacher, *The Christian Faith,* ed. H. R. MacKintosh and J. S. Stewart (New York and Evanston, 1963), I, 12–18.
31. Rudolph Otto, *The Idea of the Holy,* trans. John W. Harvey (London, 1959), pp. 26–27.
32. A consideration and analysis of these positions in the American theological scene is succinctly presented by Carl Michalson, "Is American Theology Coming of Age?" *The Drew Gateway,* XXXVI (Spring–Summer, 1966), 65–75.
33. Lawrence Ferlinghetti, "Sometime during Eternity," *A Coney Island of the Mind* (New York, 1958), pp. 15–16.
34. Ferlinghetti, "Big Fat Hairy Vision of Evil," *Penguin Modern Poets Five* (London, 1963), p. 60.
35. Quoted in Alan W. Watts, *The Way of Zen* (New York: 1959), p. 116.
36. Alan Watts, *Beat Zen, Square Zen, and Zen* (San Francisco, 1959), pp. 7–8.
37. *Ibid.,* p. 3.
38. John Clellan Holmes, "The Philosophy of the Beat Generation," *op. cit.* (above, note 19), p. 15.
39. Erich Fromm, *Psychoanalysis and Religion,* New Haven, 1959), p. 22.
40. Alan Watts, *Beat Zen, Square Zen, and Zen, op. cit.,* p. 5.
41. *Ibid.,* p. 9.
42. Watts, *op. cit.* (above, note 36).
43. *Beat Zen, Square Zen, and Zen, op. cit.,* Foreword.
44. *Ibid.*

45. Watts, *The Way of Zen*, p. 40.

46. "Poetry, Violence, and the Trembling Lambs," *The Village Voice*, IV (August 25, 1959), 8.

47. Quoted from the poem "He", dedicated to Allen Ginsberg, reprinted in *The New American Poetry, op. cit.*, pp. 134–37.

48. *Ibid.*, pp. 134–35.

49. "Poetry, Violence, and the Trembling Lambs," *op. cit.* (above, note 46), I, 8.

50. James Dickey, "From Babel to Byzantium," *Sewanee Review*, LXV (Summer, 1957), 509.

51. James Scully, Review of *Reality Sandwiches, Nation*, CXCVII (November 16, 1963), 330.

52. *Ibid.*

53. *The New American Poetry, op. cit.*, pp. 437–38.

54. *Howl and Other Poems*, p. 8.

55. Richard Kostelanetz, "Ginsberg Makes the World Scene," *New York Times*, VI (July 11, 1965), 27.

56. *Ibid.*, 28.

57. *Ibid.*

58. *Ibid.*, 30.

59. Letter by Ginsberg dated November 22, 1966.

60. "*Kral Majales*," "*The New Writing in the U.S.A.*, ed. Donald Allen and Robert Creeley (Aylesbury, 1967), p. 97.

61 Landon Y. Jones, Jr., " 'Response' 1966," *Princeton Alumni Weekly*, LXVI (May 17, 1966), 8.

62. *New York Times*, VI (July 11, 1965), 27.

Chapter Two

1. Thomas Parkinson, "Phenomenon or Generation," *A Casebook on the Beat*, ed. Thomas Parkinson (New York, 1961), p. 287.

2. Quoted in "Beat Zen, Square Zen, and Zen," *Chicago Review* (Summer, 1958), p. 8; and Carl Michalson, *Worldly Theology* (New York, 1967), p. 189.

3. *Walt Whitman's Poems*, ed. Gay Wilson Allen and Charles T. Davis (New York, 1955), p. 87.

4. A. R. Ammons, "Ginsberg's New Poems," *Poetry*, CIV (June, 1964), 186–87.

5. Robert Duncan, quoted in *The New Writing in the U.S.A.*, ed. Donald Allen and Robert Creeley (Aylesbury, 1967), p. 18.

6. "The Art of Poetry VIII," *op. cit.* (above, Chapter One, note 16), 21.

7. John Ciardi, "Epitaph for Dead Beats," *Saturday Review* (February 6, 1960), 13.

8. Watts, *Beat Zen, Square Zen, and Zen, op. cit.*, p. 12.

9. Ciardi, "Epitaph for Dead Beats," *op. cit.*, 12.

10. William Burroughs, *The New Writing in the U.S.A., op. cit.*, p. 20.

11. Francis Golffing and Barbara Gibbs, "The Public Voice: Remarks on Poetry Today—The Reality of Verse," *Commentary*, 28 (July, 1959), 66.

12. See, for example, "The Art of Poetry VIII," *op. cit.*, 12, 22.

13. Karl Shapiro, *A Primer for Poets* (Lincoln, Neb., 1953), p. 46.

14. "The Art of Poetry VIII," *op. cit.*, 28–29.

15. Erich Auerbach, *Mimesis* (Garden City, N.Y., 1957), pp. 1–20.

16. See Alan W. Watts, *Beat Zen, Square Zen, and Zen, op. cit.*, pp. 12–15.

17. *Ibid.*, p. 13.

18. Carl D. Michalson, *The Rationality of Faith* (New York, 1963), p. 88.

19. Ciardi, "Epitaph for Dead Beats," *op. cit.*, 13.

20. William Carlos Williams, "Preface to 'The Wedge,'" *Selected Essays* (New York, 1954).

21. LeRoi Jones, Introduction to *The Moderns*, ed. LeRoi Jones (London, 1965), p. ix.

22. William Carlos Williams, *I Wanted to Write a Poem, ed.* Edith Heal (Boston, 1958), p. 15.

23. Charles Olson, "Projective Verse," *The New American Poetry*, ed. Donald M. Allen (New York and London, 1960), pp. 389–90.

24. William Carlos Williams, "Essay on *Leaves of Grass*," *Leaves of Grass One Hundred Years After*, ed. Hindus (Stanford, 1955), p. 23.

25. Olson, "Projective Verse," *op. cit.*, p. 387.

26. "Notes for *Howl and Other Poems*" (Fantasy 7006, 1959), reprinted in *The New American Poetry, op. cit.*, pp. 415–16.

27. "The Art of Poetry VIII," *op. cit.*, 22.

28. "Notes for *Howl and Other Poems*," *op. cit.*, 414–15.

29. See *Paris Review* interview: "The Art of Poetry VIII," pp. 52–53.

30. Jack Kerouac, "Essentials of Spontaneous Prose," *Evergreen Review*, II (Summer, 1958), 72.

31. "Notes for *Howl and Other Poems*," *op. cit.*, p. 415.

32. "The Art of Poetry VIII," *op. cit.*, 20.

33. Kerouac, "Essentials of Spontaneous Prose," *Evergreen Review*, II (Summer, 1958), 72.

34. Kenneth Rexroth, "Disengagement: The Art of the Beat Generation," *New World Writing No. 11* (New York: The New American Library, 1957), p. 39.

35. Olson, "Projective Verse," *The New American Poetry, op. cit.*, p. 387.

36. John MacQuarrie, *God-Talk: An Examination of the Language and Logic of Theology* (London, 1967), p. 240.
37. Carl Michalson, *The Rationality of Faith* (New York, 1963), p. 115.
38. This could account for James Dickey's remark that "Ginsberg is the perfect inhabitant, if not the very founder of Babel, where conditions do not so much make tongues incomprehensible, but render their utterances, as poetry, meaningless." *Sewanee Review,* LXV (Summer, 1957), 509.
39. Norman Podhoretz, "The Know-nothing Bohemians," *Partisan Review,* XXV (Spring, 1958), 308.
40. Carl Michalson, *The Rationality of Faith,* p. 115. Compare this with Ginsberg's remark: "The rhythm of the long line is also an animal cry." "The Art of Poetry VIII," *op. cit.,* 23.
41. "The Public Voice: Remarks on Poetry Today—The Reality of Verse," *op. cit.,* pp. 67–68.
42. Carl Michalson, *The Rationality of Faith,* p. 117.
43. William Carlos Williams, *Paterson I, op. cit.*
44. Olson, "Projective Verse," *op. cit.,* 387.
45. C. E. Pulos, *The New Critics and the Language of Poetry,* University of Nebraska Studies, No. 19 (Lincoln, 1958), p. 13.
46. Yvor Winters, "The Experimental School in American Poetry," *In Defense of Reason* (1947), reprinted in *Discussions of Poetry: Form and Structure,* ed. Francis Murphy (Boston, 1964), p. 32.
47. "The Art of Poetry VIII," *op. cit.,* 22–24.
48. Robert Hazel, review of *Empty Mirror, Nation,* CXCIII (November 11, 1961), 381.
49. Shapiro, *A Primer for Poets, op. cit.,* p. 26.
50. Williams, Introduction to *Howl and Other Poems* (San Francisco, 1956), p. 7.

Chapter Three

1. Quoted in *The Indianapolis Star* (October 23, 1961).
2. Dante Gabriel Rossetti, *The House of Life,* "The Sonnet."
3. Paul Tillich, *The Courage to Be* (New Haven, 1952), p. 147.
4. Nikolai Berdyaev, *Dream and Reality: An Essay in Autobiography,* reprinted in *A Casebook on Existentialism,* ed. William V. Spanos (New York, 1966), p. 319.
5. *Hamlet,* III. i. 79.
6. See above, note 3.
7. William V. Spanos, "Abraham, Sisyphus, and the Furies: Some Introductory Notes on Existentialism," *A Casebook on Existentialism, op. cit.,* p. 5.
8. Berdyaev, *Dream and Reality, op. cit.,* p. 322.

9. "The Art of Poetry VIII," *op. cit.*, 37.
10. *Ibid.*, 49.
11. *Ibid.*, 48.
12. *Op. cit.*, p. 321.
13. "The Art of Poetry VIII," *op. cit.*, 35.
14. Lïbuse Lukas Miller, *In Search of the Self: The Individual in the Thought of Kierkegaard* (Philadelphia, 1961), p. 120.
15. "The Art of Poetry VIII,'" *op. cit.*, 24–25.
16. Paul Tillich, "Existentialist Aspects of Modern Art," *Christianity and the Existentialists,* ed. Carl Michalson (New York, 1956), p. 137.
17. "The Art of Poetry VIII," *op. cit.*, 30.
18. Quoted by Ginsberg in "The Art of Poetry," *op. cit.*, 28.
19. Tillich, *Dynamics of Faith* (New York 1958), p. 1.
20. *Ibid.*, p. 6.
21. "The Art of Poetry VIII," *op. cit.*, 30.
22. Quoted in *The New Writing in the U.S.A., op. cit.*, p. 20.
23. Paul Tillich, "Existentialist Aspects of Modern Art," *op. cit.*, p. 137.
24. Robert Hazel, Review of *Empty Mirror, Nation,* CXCIII (November 11, 1961), 381.
25. "The Art of Poetry VIII," *op. cit.*, 41.
26. Albert Camus, "Absurd Freedom," *The Myth of Sisyphus and Other Essays* (New York, 1955), reprinted in *A Casebook on Existentialism, op. cit.*, p. 298.
27. *Song of Myself,* xxiii, 480.
28. Norman Mailer, "The White Negro," *Dissent* (Summer, 1957), reprinted in *Protest,* ed. Gene Feldman and Max Gartenberg (Aylesbury, 1960), p. 289.
29. *Song of Myself,* xxiii, 480f.
30. Erich Dinkler, "Martin Heidegger," *Christianity and The Existentialists, op. cit.*, p. 110.
31. *Ibid.*, p. 109.
32. Mailer, "The White Negro," *op. cit.*, 289.
33. Wallace Stevens, "The Comedian as the Letter C," Part I, lines 1–4.
34. A measure of the extent of this derailment can be gauged by noting this portion of a letter from William Carlos Williams to Norman MacLeod: "When I say, and some well-meaning critic attacks my intelligence for saying it, that art has nothing to do with metaphysics —I am aiming at the very core of the matter. Art is some sort of honest answer, the forms of art, the discovery of the new in art forms —but to mix that with metaphysics is the prime intellectual offense of my day." William Carlos Williams, *Selected Essays, op. cit.*, pp. 238–239.

35. Stevens "The Sense of the Sleight-of-hand Man," lines 1–3.

36. See B. Hunsberger, "Kit Smart's Howl," *Wisconsin Studies in Comtemporary Literature,* VI (Winter, 1965), 34–44. Also, "The Art of Poetry," *op. cit.*, 17.

37. This might be contrasted with Irving Feldman's comment on Kerouac's style: "Kerouac's pace is quick enough to develop an inane liveliness, reminiscent of a person juggling his knee to some unheard music; we might call it 'cool' dithyramb." *Commentary,* XXVI (December, 1958), 544.

38. Berdyaev, *Dream and Reality, op. cit.*, pp. 321–22.

Chapter Four

1. Kenneth Rexroth, *Assays* (New York, 1961), p. 194.

2. Lawrence Ferlinghett, "Horn on *Howl,*" *Evergreen Review,* I, No. 4, p. 155.

3. Quoted from the San Francisco *Chronicle* in "Horn on *Howl,*" *ibid.*, 145.

4. *Ibid.*, 146.

5. *Ibid.*, 147.

6. Included are statements given by: Henry Rago, editor of *Poetry:* William Hogan of the San Francisco *Chronicle;* Robert Ducan and Director Ruth Witt-Diamant of the San Francisco State College Poetry Center; Thomas Parkinson, University of California; James Laughlin, New Directions; Kenneth Patchen; Northern California Booksellers Association; Barney Rosset and Donald Allen, editors of the *Evergreen Review.* The actual statements during the trial of Dr. Mark Shorer, Dr. Leo Lowenthal, Herbert Blau, Vincent McHugh, Dr. Mark Linenthal and Kenneth Rexroth.

7. See "Horn on *Howl,*" *op. cit.*, 145–58.

8. *Ibid.*, 151–52.

9. *Ibid.*, 154.

10. Fantasy, Spoken Word Series, 7006. Reprinted in *A Casebook on the Beat,* ed. Thomas Parkinson (New York, 1961), pp. 27–28.

11. "The Art of Poetry VIII," *op. cit.*, 15.

12. *Ibid.*, 15–16.

13. Fantasy, Spoken Word Series, 7006. Reprinted in *A Casebook on the Beat, op. cit.*, p. 26.

14. Yvor Winters, "The Experimental School in American Poetry," *In Defense of Reason* (1937). Reprinted in *Discussions of Poetry: Form and Structure,* ed. Francis Murphy (Boston, 1964), p. 14.

15. See "Notes Written on Finally Recording *Howl,*" *op. cit.*, 27–30.

16. *Ibid.*, 27.

17. *Village Voice,* IV (Wednesday, August 25, 1959), 8.

18. "Notes written on Finally Recording *Howl,*" *op. cit.*, 28.

19. Gay Wilson Allen, "Walt Whitman: The Search for a 'Democratic' Structure," *Walt Whitman Handbook* (New York, 1962). Reprinted in *Discussions of Poetry: Form and Structure, op. cit.*, p. 71.

20. *Ibid.*, p. 63.

21. E. C. Ross, "Whitman's Verse," *Modern Language Notes*, XLV (June, 1930), 363–64.

22. "Notes Written on Finally Recording *Howl*," *op. cit.*, 28.

23. "Notes Written on Finally Recording *Howl*," *op. cit.*, 28–29.

24. "The Art of Poetry VIII," *op. cit.*, 28.

25. "Notes on Finally Recording *Howl*," *op. cit.*, 28.

26. "The Art of Poetry VIII," *op. cit.*, 23–24.

27. *Ibid.*

28. *Ibid.*, 24.

29. This point is explained by Ginsberg in the *Paris Review* interview: "The Art of Poetry VIII," *op. cit.*, 40.

30. As Ginsberg explains it, "Part I [is] a lament for the Lamb in America. . . . Part II names the monster of mental consciousness that preys on the Lamb." "Notes Written on Finally Recording *Howl*," *op. cit.*, 29.

31. Karl Shapiro, *In Defense of Ignorance* (New York, 1965), p. 71.

32. See above, note 30.

33. "Notes Written on Finally Recording *Howl*," *op. cit.*, 29.

34. "The Art of Poetry VIII," *op. cit.*, 53.

35. *Ibid.*

36. Alan Watts, *The Way of Zen* (New York, 1957), p. 176.

37. *Ibid.*, p. 171.

38. *Ibid.*

39. *Ibid.*

40. *Ibid.*

41. *Ibid.*, p. 192.

42. Quoted in Watts, p. 187.

Chapter Five

1. Quoted in *The New York Times*, VI (July 11, 1965), 30.

2. D. Z. Phillips, *The Concept of Prayer* (London, 1965), p. 61.

3. Carl Michalson, *The Rationality of Faith* (New York, 1963), p. 85.

4. Norman Mailer, "The White Negro," reprinted in *Protest, op. cit.*, 289.

5. *The Mourner's Kaddish*, to be spoken by Reader and Mourners. I am indebted to Miss Carole Frankel of Philadelphia, Pennsylvania, for supplying this translation.

6. *The New Writing in the U.S.A.* (Aylesbury, 1967), pp. 89–96.

7. "The Art of Poetry VIII," *op. cit.*, 49.
8. *Ibid.*, 49–50.
9. *Ibid.*, 24.
10. *Ibid.*, 47.
11. Emily Dickinson, "Apparently with No Surprise," reprinted in *A Comprehensive Anthology of American Poetry*, ed. Conrad Aiken (New York, 1944), p. 177.
12. Jean-Paul Sartre, *Nausea*. Reprinted in Carl Michalson, *The Rationality of Faith*, *op. cit.*, p. 85.
13. "The Art of Poetry VIII," *op. cit.*, 39.
14. *Ibid.*, 38.
15. *Ibid.*, 37.
16. *Ibid.*, 40.
17. Ginsberg perhaps comes close to Kierkegaard here, who wrote: "The essential determination of human existence, [is] that man is an individual, and as such is both himself and the whole race, so that the whole race participates in the individual and the individual in the whole race. . . . The perfecting of the individual in himself is at the same time, and in so doing, the perfect participation in the whole." (*Der Begriff der Angst*, p. 22. Quoted in Emil Brunner, *Man in Revolt*, trans. Olive Wyon [Philadelphia, 1947]), p. 52.
18. "The Art of Poetry VIII," *op. cit.*, 38.
19. See back cover of *Kaddish and Other Poems*, 5th ed. (San Francisco, 1966).
20. See also "The Art of Poetry VIII," *op. cit.*, 39.
21. Allen Ginsberg, "Quo Vadis," *Mademoiselle Magazine* (January, 1960). Quoted by Carolyn Gaiser in "Gregory Corso: A Poet, the Beat Way," *A Casebook on the Beat*, *op. cit.*, p. 271.
22. Erich Fromm, *Psychoanalysis and Religion* (New Haven, 1959), p. 23.
23. Paul Tillich, *Dynamics of Faith* (New York, 1957), p. 9.
24. "The Art of Poetry VIII," *op. cit.*, 45.
25. *The Poems of John Donne*, ed. H. J. C. Grierson, 2nd ed., 2 vols. (Oxford, 1951), I, 369.
26. Letter to William Burroughs dated June 10, 1960 from Pucallpa, Peru. Reprinted in *The Yage Letters*, William Burroughs and Allen Ginsberg (San Francisco, 1963), p. 51.
27. *Ibid.*, p. 52.
28. "The Art of Poetry VIII," *op. cit.*, 48.
29. *Ibid.*, 47.
30. Shapiro, *A Primer for Poets*, *op. cit.*, pp. 59–60.

Chapter Six

1. William Burroughs, *Evergreen Review,* IV (January–February, 1960), 15.
2. Letter from Allen Ginsberg to this author, November 22, 1966.
3. William Carlos Williams, *Paterson II* (New York, 1948).
4. John Ciardi, "How Free Is Verse?" *Saturday Review* (October 11, 1958), 38.
5. William Carlos Williams, *I Wanted to Write a Poem,* ed. Edith Heal (Boston, 1958), p. 92.
6. Alan W. Watts, *The Way of Zen* (New York, 1959), p. 173.
7. John MacQuarrie, *Studies in Christian Existentialism* (Philadelphia, c. 1965), pp. 48–49.
8. "The Art of Poetry VIII," *Paris Review,* XXXVII (Spring, 1966), 40.
9. See *ibid.,* 22.
10. *Song of Myself.* I, 1–3; III, 40–43, 53–54.
11. James Scully [Review of *Reality Sandwiches*], *Nation,* CXCVII (November 16, 1963), 330.
12. Walt Whitman, *Song of Myself,* XX, 403–405.
13. *Ibid.,* VII, 145–47.
14. "The Sunne Rising."
15. *Times Literary Supplement,* CCXII (September 20, 1963), 706.
16. *Ibid.*
17. Norman MacCaig, "Poemburgers," [Review of *Reality Sandwiches*] *New Statesman,* LXVI (July 5, 1963), 20.
18. *Ibid.*
19. *Ibid.*
20. James Scully, [Review of *Reality Sandwiches*], *op. cit.,* 330.
21. George Poulet, *Studies in Human Time* (New York, 1959), p. 342.
22. Walt Whitman, *The Complete Poetry and Prose,* ed. M. Cowley (New York, 1948), II, 92.
23. *Ibid.,* I, 249.
24. *Times Literary Supplement* [Review of *Reality Sandwiches*], *op. cit.,* 706.
25. Scully, [Review of *Reality Sandwiches*] *Nation,* CXCVII (November 16, 1963), 330.
26. *Song of Myself,* XXIV, 524–26.
27. Allen Ginsberg, "The Change: Kyoto-Tokyo Express, July 18, 1963," *The New Writing in the U.S.A.,* ed. Donald Allen and Robert Creeley (Harmondsworth, Middlesex, England, 1967), pp. 89–96.
28. "The Art of Poetry VIII," *op. cit.,* 50.
29. *Ibid.,* 48.

30. William Burroughs and Allen Ginsburg, *The Yage Letters* (San Francisco, 1963), p. 52.
31. *Ibid.*, p. 55.
32. *Ibid.*, p. 60.
33. "The Art of Poetry VIII," *op. cit.*, 49.
34. *Ibid.*, 49.
35. *Ibid.*, 50.
36. *Song of Myself*, XXX, 648–52.
37. "The Change," *op. cit.*, 94.
38. "The Art of Poetry VIII," *op. cit.*, 51.
39. *The New Writing in the U.S.A.*, *op. cit.*, pp. 97–99.
40. San Francisco, c. 1966; published by James Koller and distributed by City Lights Publishing Company.
41. Karl Shapiro, *A Primer for Poets* (Lincoln, Neb., 1953), p. 26.

Chapter Seven

1. Kenneth Rexroth, "Disengagement: The Art of the Beat Generation," *New World Writing No. 11* (New York, 1957), p. 37.
2. Paul O'Neil, "The Only Rebellion Around," *Life*, XLVII (November 30, 1959), 126.
3. Karl Shapiro, *A Primer for Poets* (Lincoln, Neb., 1953), p. 16.
4. *Ibid.*, p. 30.
5. Quoted in "What Is Art Today?" *Time* "Essay," *Time Magazine* (January 27, 1967), 31.
6. Thomas Parkinson, "Phenomenon or Generation," *A Casebook on the Beat* (New York, 1961), p. 280.
7. Harvey Cox, "An Open Letter to Allen Ginsberg," *Commonweal* (April 21, 1967), 147–49.
8. Kenneth Rexroth, *Nation*, CLXXXIV (February 23, 1957), 159–162.
9. James Dickey, "From Babel to Byzantium," *Sewanee Review*, LXV (Summer, 1957), 509.
10. John Sisk, "Beatniks and Tradition," *Commonweal*, LXX (April 17, 1959), 77.
11. Charles Olson, "Projective Verse," reprinted in *The New American Poetry*, ed. Donald M. Allen (New York, c. 1960), p. 387.
12. *Ibid.*, pp. 387–88.
13. Shapiro, *op. cit.*, pp. 16–17.
14. Parkinson, *op. cit.*, p. 287.
15. L. S. Dembo, *Conceptions of Reality in Modern American Poetry* (Berkeley and Los Angeles, 1966), p. 217.
16. "Form is not different from emptiness, emptiness not different from form. Form is the emptiness, emptiness the form."
17. Dembo, *op. cit.*, p. 218.

18. Arthur Rimbaud, "Letters to Paul Demeney: 1871," *Prose Poems from The Illuminations,* trans. Louise Varèse (New York, 1946), pp. xxvi–xxvii.
19. *Reality Sandwiches,* p. 71.

Selected Bibliography

PRIMARY SOURCES

The following list is by no means exhaustive. It contains only the most important collections of Ginsberg's poetry along with a few single items of special significance. For a more complete listing of the hundreds of poems printed in magazines and broadsides of every variety, the reader is directed to the *Index to Little Magazines*. The items are arranged in chronological order of publication.

Howl and Other Poems. Pocket Poets Series, No. 4. San Francisco: City Lights Books, 1956.

"Ready to Roll," *Partisan Review*, XXV (Winter, 1958), 85.

"Death to Van Gogh's Ear," *Times Literary Supplement* (November 6, 1959), xii.

"Poetry, Violence and the Trembling Lambs" [Essay], *The Village Voice*, IV (August 25, 1959), 1, 8.

"Notes Written on Finally Recording *Howl*." Fantasy Records, Spoken Word Series, 7006, 1959.

Kaddish and Other Poems 1958–1960. Pocket Poets Series, No. 14. San Francisco: City Lights Books, 1961.

Empty Mirror: Early Poems. New York: Totem Press in association with Corinth Books, c. 1961.

The Yage Letters [with William Burroughs]. San Francisco: City Lights Books, c. 1963.

Reality Sandwiches. Pocket Poets Series, No. 18. San Francisco: City Lights Books, c. 1963.

"Today," *Yale Literary Magazine*, CXXXIII (New Haven, April, 1965), 55–58.

"Discovery of a New Kick" [letter]. *Esquire*, 64 (December, 1965), 151.

"The Art of Poetry VIII" [Interview with Thomas Clark]. *Paris Review*, XXXVII (Spring, 1966), 13–61.

"Fragment 1957—The Names," *Paris Review*, 37 (Spring, 1966), 57–61.

"To the Angels." Delivered as a speech at San Jose State College, Monday, November 15, 1965, before students and representatives of Bay Area Hell's Angels. *Liberation.* Reprinted in Hunter S. Thompson, *Hell's Angels,* New York: Random House, 1967.

"The Change: Kyoto–Tokyo Express, July 18, 1963." *The New Writing in the U.S.A.,* ed. Donald Allen and Robert Creeley, Harmondsworth, Middlesex, England: Penguin Books Ltd., 1967.

"Kral Majales," The New Writing in the U.S.A., op. cit.

Wichita Vortex Sutra. San Francisco: Coyote Books (distributed by City Lights Books), 1967.

Planet News. San Francisco: City Lights Books, 1968.

T.V. Baby Poems. New York: Grossman, The Orion Press, 1968.

Anthologies

ALLEN, DONALD M., ed. *The New American Poetry, 1945–1960.* New York: Grove Press, 1960.

ALLEN, DONALD and ROBERT CREELEY, eds. *The New Writing in the U.S.A.* Harmondsworth, Middlesex, England: Penguin Books Ltd., 1967.

FELDMAN, GENE and MAX GARTENBERG, eds. *The Beat Generation and the Angry Young Men.* New York: Citadel Press, 1958. Printed in Great Britain under title *Protest.* London: Panther Books, Ltd., 1960.

FERLINGHETTI, LAWRENCE, ed. *Beatitude Anthology.* San Francisco: City Lights Books, 1960.

JONES, LEROI. *The Moderns.* London: MacGibbon and Kee, 1965.

KRIM, SEYMOUR, ed. *The Beats.* New York: Fawcett Publications, Inc., 1960.

PARKINSON, THOMAS, ed. *A Casebook on the Beat.* New York: Thomas Y. Crowell Company, 1961.

Penguin Modern Poets 5, Harmondsworth, Middlesex, England: Penguin Books Ltd., 1963.

WILENTZ, ELIAS, ed. *The Beat Scene.* New York: Citadel Press/Corinth Books, Inc., 1960.

SECONDARY SOURCES

AMMONS, R. S. "Ginsberg's New Poems," *Poetry,* CIV (June, 1964), 186–87. A brief and sympathetic discussion of Ginsberg's poetic theory.

"Big Day for Bards at Bay," *Life,* XLIII (September 9, 1957), 105–108. Comments on the obscenity trial of *Howl* as well as several poets of the San Francisco Renaissance.

BINGHAM, June. "The Intelligent Square's Guide to Hippieland," *The*

New York Times Magazine, VI (September 24, 1967), 25, 68–73, 76–84. General treatment of the "Hip" and "Beat" movements; special emphasis on religious significance. Contains a few good remarks on Ginsberg's social influence.

"California's Young Writers, Angry and Otherwise." *Library Journal,* LXXXIII (June 15, 1958), 1850–54. General discussion of the major "Beat" writers with a brief biography and commentary on Ginsberg and *Howl.*

CARROLL, PAUL. *Evergreen Review,* V (July–August, 1961), 114. Favorable review of *Kaddish.*

CIARDI, JOHN. "Epitaph for the Dead Beats," *Saturday Review,* XLIII (February 6, 1960), 11–13. As the title implies, a jaundiced look at the more extreme affectations of "Beat" literature. Useful and informative despite its unsympathetic stance.

COX, HARVEY. "An Open Letter to Allen Ginsberg," *Commonweal* (April 21, 1967), 147–49. Theologian's reply to Ginsberg's challenging query: What is religion doing to make itself relevant to America today?

DICKEY, JAMES. "From Babel to Byzantium," *Sewanee Review,* LXV (Summer, 1957), 509–10. More or less hostile review that insists Ginsberg lacks craft.

———. *New York Times Book Review* (July 9, 1961), 14. Flip, unfavorable review of *Kaddish.* Refuses to recognize any poetic merit in Ginsberg.

ECKMAN, FREDERICK. "Neither Tame nor Fleecy," *Poetry,* XC (September, 1957), 386–97. Description rather than a criticism of *Howl;* concludes "it is a very shaggy book."

ERLICH, J. W., ed. *Howl of the Censor.* San Carlos, Calif.: Nourse Publishing Co., 1961. Reprint of transcript of the *Howl* obscenity trial.

FARRELL, B. "Guru Comes to Kansas," *Life,* LX (May 27, 1966), 78–80. Account of Ginsberg's poetry readings in the Midwest. Contains concluding passages from *Wichita Vortex Sutra.*

"Fried Shoes; Beatniks," *Time,* LXXIII (February 9, 1959), 16. Somewhat snide, condescending account of Ginsberg, Corso, and Orlovsky in Chicago.

FULLER, J. G. "Tradewinds," *Saturday Review,* XL (October 5, 1957), 5–7. Appraisal of the San Francisco scene just after the *Howl* trial. Sees the ridiculousness of the case against *Howl.*

GOLD, HERBERT. "The Beat Mystique." *The Beats.* Ed. Seymour Krim. New York: Fawcett Publications, 1960. Somewhat chiding exposition of the "Beat" attitude.

GOLFFING, FRANCIS and BARBARA GIBBS. "The Public Voice: Remarks on Poetry Today," *Commentary,* XXVIII (July, 1959), 63–69. Mature, intelligent attempt to place Ginsberg and other recent American poets into a traditional perspective. Extremely valuable commentary.

GROSSMAN, ALLEN. "Allen Ginsberg: The Jew as an American Poet," *Judaism,* XI, 303–8. Ethnic approach to Ginsberg's work.

HASELMAYER, LOUIS A. "Beat Prophet and Beat Wit," *Iowa English Yearbook,* No. 6 (1961), 9–13.

HAZEL, ROBERT. *Nation,* CXCII (November 11, 1961), 381. Review of *Empty Mirror;* not unfriendly but complains of Ginsberg's "strenuously induced mysticism."

HUNSBERGER, B. "Kit Smart's Howl," *Wisconsin Studies in Contemporary Literature,* VI (Winter, 1965), 34–44. Explores Ginsberg's indebtedness to Christopher Smart.

IGNATOW, DAVID. *New Leader,* XLIII (July 31 and August 7, 1961), 21. Review of *Kaddish.*

JACOBSON, D. "America's Angry Young Men: How Rebellious Are the San Francisco Rebels?" *Commentary,* XXIV (December, 1957), 475–79. Another look at the San Francisco "Beat" movement.

JONES, LANDON Y., JR. "Response 1966," *Princeton Alumni Weekly,* LXVI (May 17, 1966), 6–9. Princeton student's impressions of a Ginsberg's reading in the Ivy League.

KOSTELANETZ, RICHARD. "Ginsberg Makes the World Scene," *New York Times Magazine* (July 11, 1965), 22–23. Report of Ginsberg's journey to Prague and his subsequent crowning there as "King of May" by students.

KOTLOWITZ, R. "Performing Arts: *Kaddish* on Record," *Harper's,* CCXXXIII (October, 1966), 134–35. Review of Ginsberg's LP reading of *Kaddish.* The reaction is mixed. Reviewer criticizes Ginsberg's reading voice, but calls the experience "unforgettable." Praises poem in spite of its many flaws.

KRIM, SEYMOUR. "A Hungry Mental Lion," IV, 11 *Evergreen Review,* 178–85. Friendly look at Ginsberg's work.

LEVI, PETER. *Spectator,* No. 7017 (August 9, 1963), 179. Review of *Reality Sandwiches.*

MACCAIG, NORMAN, "Poemburgers," *New Statesman,* LXV (July 5, 1963), 20. Appreciative review of *Reality Sandwiches;* admires the strenuous energy of the poems but distrusts their "pumping up" and lack of syntax.

MCFADDEN, J. P. "Howling in the Wilderness," *National Review,* VII (September 12, 1959), 338–39. Conservative opinion on Ginsberg's extravagance in *Howl.*

MCHUGH, VINCENT. *San Francisco Chronicle,* "This World" Magazine, XXV (August 27, 1961), 26. Review of *Kaddish.*

"New Test for Obscenity." *Nation,* CLXXXV (November 9, 1957), 314. Short notice on the court decision on *Howl.*

OPPEN, GEORGE. *Poetry,* C (August, 1961), 329. Review of *Kaddish.* Finds other poems in the volume of uneven quality; sees *Kaddish* itself as "firm and significant."

PARKINSON, THOMAS. "Phenomenon or Generation." *A Casebook on the Beat.* Ed. Thomas Parkinson. New York: Thomas Y. Crowell, 1961. Most valuable assessment of the Beat poets containing sympathetic and intelligent remarks on Ginsberg's contribution.

PERLMAN, D. "How Captain Hanrahan Made *Howl* a Bestseller," *Reporter,* XVII (December 12, 1957), 20. Comment on the promotional notoriety of Ginsberg's bestseller.

PODHORETZ, NORMAN. "Howl of Protest in San Francisco," *New Republic,* CXXXVII (September 16, 1957), 20. Hostile appraisal of "Beat" literary presumptions. Some praise for *Howl.*

———. "The Know-Nothing Bohemians," *Partisan Review,* XXV (Spring, 1958), 305–11, 313–16, 318. Caustic jibes at the philosophical pretensions of Bohemia.

PRITCHETT, V. S. "The Beat Generation," *New Statesman* (September 6, 1958), 292, 294. Somewhat condescending but informative appraisal of Ginsberg, Kerouac, and other advocates of the "Beat" attitude.

REXROTH, KENNETH. "A Hope for Poetry," *Holiday Magazine* (March, 1966), 147–51. Some observations on where the New American poets are going. Short reappraisal of Ginsberg is contained in the article.

———. "Disengagement: The Art of the Beat Generation," *New World Writing No. 11.* New York: The New American Library, 1957. One of the first early serious considerations of "Beat" literature. Urbane, erudite, and of first significance.

———. "The New American Poets," *Harper's Magazine* (June, 1965), 65–71. A general comment on recent American poetry with some fine tributes paid to *Howl* in particular.

———. *Nation,* 184 (February 23, 1957), 159–62. Sees Ginsberg's poetry as technically representing the first attempt since Sandburg to handle American rhythms in long strophic lines, but warns that Ginsberg runs the risk of becoming a popular entertainer.

ROSENBERG, HAROLD. *Commentary,* XXXI (October, 1961), 349. Short, incisive review of *Kaddish;* generally appreciative.

ROSENTHAL, MOCHA L. *The New American Poetry.* New York: Macmillan, 1967. Devotes a chapter to Ginsberg; an excellent assessment of the poet's significance.

———. "Poet of the New Violence," *Nation,* CLXXXIV (February 23, 1957), 162. Favorable review of *Howl.*

———. "Poet and Public Figure," *New York Times Book Review* (August 14, 1966), 4–5. Raises the issue of the new American poets, Ginsberg in particular, as social as well as literary forces.

RUMAKER, MICHAEL. "Allen Ginsberg's *Howl*," *Black Mountain Review* (Autumn, 1957), 228–37. One of the first serious, systematic considerations of Ginsberg's most popular poem. Important article.

SCULLY, JAMES. *Nation*, XCVII (November 16, 1963), 329. Sound judicious look at *Reality Sandwiches;* wisely separates the wheat from the chaff.

SHAPIRO, HARVEY. *Midstream*, VII (Autumn, 1961), 95. Review of *Kaddish.*

SISK, JOHN P. "Beatniks and Tradition," *Commonweal*, LXX (April 17, 1959), 74–77. Good solid achievement in placing "Beat" literature in historical perspective. Most valuable essay on the esthetic principles of Ginsberg and his milieu.

SPECTOR, ROBERT D. "The Poet's Other Voices, Other Rooms," *Saturday Review*, XLVII (February 1, 1964), 37. Contrasts Whitman and Ginsberg in a brief but friendly review of *Reality Sandwiches.*

STEPANCHEV, STEPHEN. "Popular Poetry: Allen Ginsberg," *American Poetry Since 1945.* New York: Harper & Row, c. 1965. This chapter devoted to Ginsberg covers the ground but casts little critical illumination that is new.

"Three Poets," *Poetry*, 100 (August, 1922), 329–31. Review of *Kaddish;* finds the title poem quite good but criticizes the others for their uneven quality.

TILLING, DIANA (pseud.). "The Other Night in Heaven," *The Fifties*, No. 3, pp. 54–56. Parody of Diana Trilling's account of a Ginsberg reading at Columbia University.

Times Literary Supplement, No. 3097 (June 30, 1961), 404. Somewhat caustic review of *Kaddish.*

Times Literary Supplement, No. 3211 (September 20, 1963), 706. Extremely hostile review of *Reality Sandwiches* which considers Ginsberg a naïve writer and a crude sentimentalist.

TRILLING, DIANA. "The Other Night at Columbia," *Partisan Review*, XXVI (Spring, 1959), 214–30. Very interesting because it gives firsthand, if subjective, appraisals of Ginsberg as a student and neophyte poet. Tells as much about Mrs. Trilling as it does about Ginsberg but is, nevertheless, informative and interesting. Rather maternal regard for Ginsberg as black sheep runs implicitly throughout the article.

WESLING, D. "Berkeley: Free Speech and Free Verse," *Nation*, XX (November 8, 1965), 338–40. Account of a reading at Berkeley by Ginsberg, Charles Olson, Robert Duncan, and Robert Creeley. The reading was held during the notorious "Free Speech Movement" on the campus; more important on philosophical matters than literary.

WHALEN, PHILIP. *San Francisco Chronicle,* "This World" Magazine (August 4, 1963), 29. Enthusiastic review of *Reality Sandwiches.*

Index